Tonal Coherence in
Mahler's Ninth Symphony

Studies in Musicology, No. 79

George Buelow, Series Editor
Professor of Music
Indiana University

Other Titles in This Series

No. 71	*The Keyboard Music of John Bull*	Walker Cunningham
No. 73	*Essays on J.S. Bach*	Gerhard Herz
No. 74	*Programmatic Elements in the Works of Schoenberg*	Walter B. Bailey
No. 75	*Music and Ritual at Papal Avignon, 1309-1403*	Andrew Tomasello
No. 76	*Brahms's Choral Compositions and His Library of Early Music*	Virginia Hancock
No. 77	*The Instrumental Music of Carl Philipp Emanuel Bach*	David Schulenberg
No. 78	*Opera Seria and the Evolution of Classical Style, 1755-1772*	Eric Weimer
No. 80	*Fundamental Bass Theory in Nineteenth Century Vienna*	Robert W. Wason

Tonal Coherence in Mahler's Ninth Symphony

by
Christopher Orlo Lewis

UMI RESEARCH PRESS
Ann Arbor, Michigan

Copyright © 1984, 1983
Christopher Orlo Lewis
All rights reserved

Produced and distributed by
UMI Research Press
an imprint of
University Microfilms International
A Xerox Information Resources Company
Ann Arbor, Michigan 48106

Library of Congress Cataloging in Publication Data

Lewis, Christopher Orlo.
Tonal coherence in Mahler's Ninth symphony.

(Studies in musicology ; no. 79)
Revision of thesis (Doctoral)–University of Rochester, Eastman School of Music, 1983.
Bibliography: p.
Includes index.
1. Mahler, Gustav, 1860-1911. Symphonies, no. 9.
I. Title. II. Series.
ML410.M23L48 1984   785.1'1'0924   84-2754
ISBN 0-8357-1585-X

For Florence

Contents

List of Examples *ix*

Acknowledgments *xvii*

1 Introduction *1*

2 *Andante Comodo* *13*

3 *Ländler* *43*

4 *Rondo-Burleske* *65*

5 Finale *101*

Notes *119*

Bibliography *125*

Index *127*

List of Examples

1.1. Double-Tonic Sonorities *6*

1.2. Chromatic Third Relationships *7*

1.3. Design of the Ninth Symphony *10*

2.1. Design of the *Andante Comodo* *13*

2.2. S.S. and Sketch, mm. 1–7 *14*

2.3. Tonal Implication of Motive "X" *15*

2.4. Sketch of mm. 7–54 *15*

2.5. Sketch of mm. 7–14 *16*

2.6. Sketch of mm. 29–36 *16*

2.7. Sketch of mm. 53–64 *17*

2.8. S.S., mm. 76–83 *18*

2.9. S.S., mm. 79–81 *19*

2.10. S.S., mm. 80–82 *19*

2.11. Sketch of mm. 80–96 *20*

2.12. Motive "Y" *21*

2.13. Tonal Plot of the Exposition *21*

x   List of Examples

2.14. Tonal Plot of the First Movement   22

2.15. Design of the Development   23

2.16. S.S., mm. 130–35   24

2.17. Sketch of mm. 148–60   24

2.18. Beginning of the Second Refrain   25

2.19. Sketch of mm. 234–37   26

2.20. Transition to Episode 4   26

2.21. Sketch of mm. 267–75   26

2.22. Sketch of mm. 108–19   27

2.23. Sketch of mm. 108–19   27

2.24. Reduction of mm. 119-23   28

2.25. Sketch of mm. 160–82   29

2.26. Sketch of mm. 182–98   29

2.27. Three Versions of the Second Theme   30

2.28. S.S., mm. 211–15   30

2.29. Sketch of mm. 219–34   31

2.30. S.S., mm. 246–50   32

2.31. Reduction of mm. 253–66   32

2.32. Sketch of mm. 277–85   33

2.33. Sketch of mm. 285–99   33

2.34. Sketch of mm. 299–310   34

2.35. Variants of Motive "X"   35

List of Examples   xi

2.36. Motive "X" in the Retransition   *35*

2.37. The Retransition   *36*

2.38. Sketch of mm. 365–71   *38*

2.39. Recapitulation of the Second Theme   *38*

2.40. Reduction and Sketch of mm. 376–91   *39*

2.41. Sketch of mm. 391–98   *39*

2.42. Reduction of mm. 414–34   *40*

3.1. Design of the Second Movement   *44*

3.2. Andraschke's Analysis   *45*

3.3. Designs of Draft and Final Versions   *46*

3.4. Key-Plan of the Second Movement   *46*

3.5. Reduction of mm. 187–205   *47*

3.6. Phrase Structure of Section 1   *48*

3.7. Plagal Prolongation, mm. 30–40   *48*

3.8. S.S., mm. 66–70 and 75–79   *49*

3.9. Themes of the Three Dances   *49*

3.10. Origin of the Motto Progression   *50*

3.11. S.S., mm. 227–31   *51*

3.12. Background, mm. 218–52   *51*

3.13. S.S., mm. 512–22   *52*

3.14. Versions of Waltz I   *53*

3.15. Sketch of mm. 90–96   *53*

3.16. Waltz in D Major 55

3.17. Transition to the Last Waltz I 56

3.18. S.S. and Sketch, mm. 486–89 56

3.19. Comparison of Draft and Final Versions 58

3.20. Reduction of mm. DS 194–278 59

3.21. Facsimile of Draft Score p. II/19 60

3.22. S.S., mm. DS 580–92 61

3.23. Motto Theme in the Last *Ländler* 62

3.24. S.S., mm. 539–53 62

3.25. Sketch of mm. 539–51 63

4.1. Design of the Third Movement 66

4.2. Design of Refrain 1 67

4.3. Sketch of mm. 1–7 67

4.4. Two Interpretations of mm. 1–2 68

4.5. Sketch of mm. 1–7 68

4.6. Sketch of mm. 7–14 69

4.7. Sketches of mm. 17–22 69

4.8. Implications of C and A in mm. 22 ff. 70

4.9. Compound Bass, mm. 26–34 70

4.10. Sketch of mm. 26–28 71

4.11. Sketch of mm. 26–28 71

4.12. S.S., mm. 28–34 72

4.13. S.S., mm. 33–34   *72*

4.14. E/C Double Tonic   *72*

4.15. S.S., mm. 34–38   *72*

4.16. Sketch of mm. 38–45   *73*

4.17. Source of mm. 56 ff.   *74*

4.18. Sketch of mm. 66–71   *74*

4.19. Sketch of mm. 71–79   *75*

4.20. S.S., mm. 84–88   *76*

4.21. Mm. 6 ff. and mm. 88 ff.   *76*

4.22. Sketch of mm. 88–101   *76*

4.23. S.S., mm. 94–96   *77*

4.24. S.S., mm. 104–8   *78*

4.25. Design of Refrain 2   *78*

4.26. Sources of Refrain 2   *79*

4.27. M. 55 Compared with m. 191   *79*

4.28. Sketch of mm. 192–99   *79*

4.29. Sketches of mm. 66–71 and mm. 199–204   *80*

4.30. Sketch of mm. 204–9   *80*

4.31. Sketch of mm. 209–27   *81*

4.32. S.S., mm. 224–27   *81*

4.33. Comparison of Strophes 3 and 4   *81*

4.34. S.S. and Sketch, mm. 244–45   *82*

List of Examples

4.35. Design of Episode 1   83

4.36. Sketch of mm. 109–20   83

4.37. Major Third Progressions   83

4.38. Sketch of mm. 147–59   84

4.39. S.S., mm. 166–69   84

4.40. S.S. and Sketches, mm. 177–79   85

4.41. Design of Episode 2   86

4.42. Sketch of mm. 262–75   86

4.43. S.S., mm. 264–67   86

4.44. S.S. and Sketch, mm. 289–96   86

4.45. Reduction of mm. 281–96   87

4.46. S.S., mm. 318–23   88

4.47. Tonal Plot of Episode 2   89

4.48. Prime Motives of Episode 3   89

4.49. Tonal Plot of Movement I   90

4.50. Design of Episode 3   91

4.51. S.S. and Sketch, mm. 348–52   91

4.52. S.S., mm. 362–68   91

4.53. S.S., mm. 380–83 and 388–94   92

4.54. S.S., mm. 434–38   92

4.55. Transition to Part 2   93

4.56. S.S., mm. 464–71   93

4.57.	Sketch of mm. 478–80	*93*
4.58.	S.S., mm. 472–75	*94*
4.59.	Transition to Refrain 3	*95*
4.60.	Approach to and Departure from Episode 3	*95*
4.61.	Key-Plan of the *Rondo-Burleske*	*96*
4.62.	Comparison of Refrains 1 and 3	*97*
4.63.	Sketch of mm. 56–62 and mm. 533–40	*97*
4.64.	Sketch of mm. 542–61	*98*
4.65.	Sketch of mm. 613–17	*98*
4.66.	Comparison of mm. 617–27 and 629–39	*98*
4.67.	Sketch of mm. 641–55 and mm. 661–67	*98*
5.1.	Tonal Connections among the Four Movements	*104*
5.2.	Tonal Plan of the Ninth Symphony	*104*
5.3.	Design of the Finale	*105*
5.4.	Two Functions of A-Flat	*106*
5.5.	Sketch of mm. 3–4 (17–18)	*107*
5.6.	Sketch of mm. 4–7	*107*
5.7.	Sketch of mm. 13–15	*107*
5.8.	D Major at Climaxes	*108*
5.9.	S.S., mm. 40–49	*109*
5.10.	Sketch of mm. 53–59	*109*
5.11.	S.S., mm. 61–64	*110*

List of Examples

5.12. Sketches of mm. 64–68 and mm. 68–73 *110*

5.13. Sketch of mm. 73–80 *111*

5.14. Openings of Episodes 1 and 2 *111*

5.15. S.S., mm. 97–101 *112*

5.16. Sketch of mm. 102–7 *112*

5.17. Sketch of mm. 107–18; Reduction of mm. 115–17 *113*

5.18. Sketch of mm. 126–30 *114*

5.19. Sketch of mm. 130–34 *115*

5.20. Sketch of mm. 138–48 *115*

5.21. Sketch of mm. 148–60 *115*

5.22. S.S., mm. 160–73 *116*

Acknowledgments

I am grateful to Universal Edition, Vienna, and European American Music Distributors Corporation, sole agent in North America for Universal Edition, for their permission to quote so extensively from the engraved score and the photographic reproduction of Mahler's orchestral draft of the Ninth Symphony.

Dr. Robert Stangeland, Chairman of the Department of Music, and Dr. Alfred Fisher, Chairman of the Theory and Composition Division of the University of Alberta, made the completion of this work possible by arranging for me to have a year free from my teaching duties. Professors David Beach, Robert Gauldin and Deborah Stein assisted the later stages of my work by their careful reading and many useful suggestions.

As is always the case with such an undertaking, colleagues and friends have given generous help. In particular I wish to thank Gordon Sly and James Doerksen, for proofreading; Henry Klumpenhouwer, for music autography; Peter Clements, for teaching me about word processing; Patrick McCreless, for many musical insights and much personal support; and Penelope Peters, for the gifts of her musicianship and her friendship.

Dr. Robert Bailey has inspired this project with his remarkably original insights into post-Wagnerian tonal structures. His provision of a framework for the intellectual appreciation of late nineteenth-century music—the sheer scope and emotional power of which have long obscured its complex tonal logic—is a theoretical innovation of the first rank. My own study could not have been conceived without his ideas, any more than it could have been carried through to completion without his guidance.

I owe to my family a great deal for their constant help. In particular I thank my brother Robin for his encouragement and cheer as we underwent the concurrent agony of our writing. My parents have given generous material and spiritual support, and in many other ways have made my road easier.

This work is dedicated to my wife, Florence, in tribute to her influence on its author, and to her own accomplishments. Having established an unsurpassable reputation in her own profession while helping me through graduate school, she is now about to publish our first child as this book goes to press—an entirely appropriate coincidence, since both productions are in many senses collaborations.

1

Introduction

In February of 1912 the publisher of Gustav Mahler's Fifth Symphony inquired of Arnold Schoenberg whether the plates for that work ought not to be melted down. Schoenberg, horrified, replied, "For God's sake, not that of all things! Young people today worship Mahler as a god. His time will come in five to ten years at most."[1] Schoenberg's artistic evaluation was of course correct, but his prediction of an imminent full appreciation of Mahler was not. Even now, seventy years later, although there is a steadily increasing popular and musicological interest in Mahler, we have still no complete scholarly biography and very few analytic studies of his music.

The relative dearth of analysis is aggravated by the concentration of the few such studies upon either motivic detective work or consideration of the programmatic meaning of the symphonies. This latter field is especially fertile since even those symphonies which do not involve direct literary statements by the inclusion of text are by no means devoid of programmatic or, rather, autobiographical and philosophical significance. Such considerations should not, however, supersede or even rival purely musical problems.

That achieving an accurate historical view of Mahler has proved so difficult may be because "the writers on the subject, even the most recent ones, are still basically nineteenth-century people, either by age or by disposition;"[2] an analytical approach to Mahler's music—as to that of his contemporaries— has certainly been hampered by the general assumption that it is still basically nineteenth-century music predicated upon the same principles that define the musical syntax of the first part of the century.[3]

Certain aspects of Mahler's music do differ from earlier practice and are therefore crucial clues to an understanding of his style. It is now usual for American and British Mahler scholars to take for granted the term "progressive tonality," coined by Dika Newlin,[4] but when it was first introduced there was considerable opposition to its use. Typically, the strongest attempt to refute the term is founded upon a stunning misinterpretation of Newlin's meaning. In a rather vitriolic article written soon after the appearance of the first edition of Newlin's book, Hans Tischler takes the adjective "progressive" to have been intended as the antonym of "conservative," and therefore meaningless as a modifier of "tonality."[5] The term is further ill-chosen, he says, because it "does not convey what Miss Newlin meant it to, namely the utilization of key symbolism for musico-dramatic purposes."[6]

Newlin clearly does not intend either of the meanings imputed to her by Tischler. She is referring simply to the device of beginning and ending a musical structure in different keys, of "progressing" from one key to another, and in this sense her term is the antonym of "concentric."[7] Further, she makes a direct statement about her view of musico-dramatic symbolism:

> We have already said that Mahler's symphonic music has strong dramatic tendencies, and that its spirit is often close to that of the Wagnerian music-drama. Now, key-consciousness in dramatic music, at least in dramatic music of the nineteenth century (for the profound and detailed key-symbolism of the *Magic Flute* is quite another matter) is of far less importance than in symphonic music. This . . . simply means that the composer, on the one hand, is much less likely to be concerned about the possible effect of several returns to the same key in an operatic scene than in a symphonic movement, and on the other hand, that even the intensely musical listener is, by the same token, equally unlikely to observe such returns to a given key or to notice whether a scene begins and ends in the same key. [Thus] . . . a tonal procedure which would have seemed unnatural, amateurish, even, in a classical symphony, is perfectly understandable in Mahler.[8]

One need not agree with Newlin's statement to allow that it has nothing to do with Tischler's incredibly naive "dramatic key-symbolism." One example, his view of the Mahler Fifth, will demonstrate that he is not concerned with a musical process: "C-sharp minor (expressing mourning and pain) — A minor (signifying tragic fighting and wounds) — D major (exposing forced, ironic gaiety) — F major (for an idyllic interlude of sad repose) — D major (representing work, haste, but courage)."[9]

That Tischler's criticisms are completely unfounded does not, however, mean that Newlin's term is ideal. In fact, it is gravely misleading, since to distinguish between "progressive" and "concentric" pieces solely according to the beginning and ending keys is to imply that Mahler's music alternates, apparently at random, between two tonal languages. It is internal syntactical relationships which define a musical language, and while progressive tonality requires a violation of certain of the rules of common practice, a violation of those rules need not necessarily produce a progressive background. Mahler's tonal procedures would be more than "unnatural and amateurish" in a classical symphony — they would be utterly impossible. It is quite clear from the Schenkerian definition of common-practice tonality that the identity of beginning and ending keys arises from a syntactical imperative rather than from the composer's choice. A common-practice piece does not just begin and end in the same key, is not simply "in" a given key, but expresses a *single tonic triad*. "All the foreground diminutions including the apparent 'keys' arising out of the voice-leading transformations, ultimately emanate from the diatony (*Ursatz*) in the background."[10] Schenker even explains several pieces with "deceptive beginnings," including the last movement of Beethoven's Fourth Piano Concerto, and the Chopin Scherzo Op. 31 in D-flat (sic) major.[11] In each of his examples, however, despite the difficulties of the beginnings, the progression establishing the actual tonic (that is, the first element of the *Ursatz*) is direct and occurs relatively early, so that the *Ursatz* itself explicitly generates the greater part of the piece.

This is not the case, however, in most late nineteenth-century works which Newlin regards as exhibiting "progressive tonality." To take only one example: the "deceptive beginning" of the Finale of the Mahler Second Symphony occupies more than 90 percent of the movement, since the earliest point at which the *Ursatz* of E-flat could be taken as beginning is m. 696 (of 764). It is true that the elements of the *Ursatz* are important because of function and not duration, and that the *Ursatz* itself is an abstraction, but an abstraction so far removed from one's perception of the piece seems of limited value. One cannot adequately describe the nature of the movement without allowing that the most important aspect of its tonal design *is* a progression from C to E-flat, and whether or not E-flat is eventually realized through a Schenkerian fundamental structure is more or less irrelevant. Schenker might well account for this by saying that such a work is in some sense incomplete,[12] but it is possible today to honor Schenker and still hold that there is music which does not conform to his model and is therefore not in essence common-practice. To put it another way, while Schenkerian analysis might find a tonal fundamental structure behind such a piece, it will be so abstract and so distorted as to be far less useful in defining the language of the work than are other aspects of the actual tonal structure. These other aspects may be considered the "tonal plot"[13] of the work.

If such a piece is to be heard as a coherent artistic entity then we must understand not just its beginning and ending, but also all the intervening material which contributes to making the one a logical outcome of the other. To return to the example of the Mahler Second, the emergence of E-flat as the concluding tonality after five movements *must* be prepared. The whole symphony, therefore, is designed around a pairing of the keys of C and E-flat. The same basic tonal plot (in simplest terms a pairing of C and E-flat) provides the framework for both "concentric" (first and third) and "progressive" (fifth) movements. Newlin's distinction between the two is at best artificial: most of the mature Mahler pieces are founded upon such a pairing of tonics, of which either may predominate at the beginning and at the same one *or* the other emerge as conclusive tonic.

The most important theoretical treatise by a composer roughly contemporary with Mahler is Schoenberg's *Theory of Harmony*. Schoenberg briefly discusses techniques related to "paired tonics" under the topics "fluctuating" and "suspended" tonality:

> Whoever wants to take a look at it [late nineteenth-century music] will find many examples in the music of Mahler and others . . .
>
> Two pregnant examples of fluctuating tonality from my own compositions are: *Orchesterlied*, Op. 8, No. 5, "Voll jener Susse," which wavers principally between D-flat and B major; and Op. 6, No. 7 (*Lied*), "Lockung," which expresses an E-flat major tonality without once in the course of the piece giving an E-flat major triad in such a way that one could regard it as pure tonic.
>
> . . . If the key is to fluctuate, it will have to be established somewhere. But not too firmly; it should be loose enough to yield.
>
> . . . Further documentation is to be found in Wagner. For example, the Prelude to *Tristan*. Note that A minor, although it is to be inferred from every passage, is scarcely ever sounded in the whole piece. It is always expressed in circuitous ways.
>
> . . . As for suspended tonality, the theme is undoubtedly the crux of the matter. It must give opportunity for such harmonic looseness through its characteristic figurations. The purely harmonic aspect will involve almost exclusive use of explicitly vagrant [i.e., tonally ambiguous] chords.[14]

Earlier in the same treatise four possible treatments of tonal digression and modulation are succinctly listed. Schoenberg's third and fourth points are:

> 3. From the outset the tonic does not appear unequivocally, it is not definitive; rather, it admits the rivalry of other tonics alongside it. The tonality is kept, so to speak, suspended, and *the victory can then go to one of the rivals, though not necessarily.*
>
> 4. The harmony is nowhere disposed to allow a tonic to assert its authority. Structures are created whose laws do not seem to issue from a central source; at least this central source is not a *single* fundamental tone.[15]

Schoenberg does not refer to these techniques as abstract theories, nor as practices of his own invention, but as compositional procedures of which there are numerous examples in the works of other composers.

In a recent paper, Robert Bailey laid the historical and theoretical groundwork for an understanding of post-Wagnerian tonal structures, saying that they are founded upon a pairing of two tonics, and that the idea of "progress" from one to the other is not essential:

> These two tonalities are not really set in opposition to each other like the contrasting keys found in earlier practice; rather, they are co-existent, in such a way as to form what I have chosen to call a double-tonic complex. Within such a complex, one key of the pair maintains a primary position, though *either one can serve as representative of the tonic.*[16]

Although any relationship between the two members of the complex is possible, a third is by far the most common interval, and always obtains before 1900. The classical affinity between major and minor relatives provides a natural basis for the more intimate association of the double-tonic complex (thus, for example: A minor/C major (*Tristan*, Act I), C/E-flat (Mahler II), G/E (Mahler IV), C/E-flat (Schoenberg, "Lockung")). Since in this music, as in that of the common practice, there is constant cross-referencing of the tonal plot from the foreground to the deeper levels (in both Schenkerian and other senses),[17] the predominance of tertially-related complexes means that especially in larger works the upper and lower thirds of the principal tonic become important, not simply as dividers or passing sonorities,[18] but as crucial secondary tonal areas in their own right. Bailey attributes the increased structural importance of the third to a diminishing of the value of the tonal contrast provided by the dominant, which becomes "closely associated with the tonic itself—often to the point of being a mere linear extension of I, or even a substitute for it."[19]

The "double-tonic complex" prescribes long-range tonal connections at a level of abstraction not so far removed from perceived surface events as is the Schenkerian *Ursatz*. But just as in classical tonality that fundamental structure may be elaborated in an infinity of ways to create the unique character of each piece, so the double-tonic complex may give rise to an immense diversity of realizations. In both styles after a certain point each piece in effect defines its own processes, and only after research has given us detailed analyses of a great many pieces can generalizations about categories of elaborational models be made. Bailey has shown, for example, that while Mahler's Fourth and *Das Lied* are both predicated upon a tertial double-tonic complex, and the earlier work is the formal model for the later, there are basic differences in even the deep background plans.

> [In the Fourth Symphony] the upper tonality of the pair, G, yields to the lower one, E. The second movement, or the second part of the first *Abteilung*, forms the primary area of tonal contrast with the other three movements, which all involve a pairing of E and G. Those other three movements are arranged in such a way that whereas G is the primary member of the complex in the first movement and for most of the third, the reversion to the primacy of E is made in the latter part of the third movement, so that E remains the [principal] tonic for the concluding movement as well.
>
> * * *
>
> [In *Das Lied*] the polarity is oriented toward the A side of the [A/C] complex in Part I (or the first five movements), while Part II shifts the polarity to the C side of the complex.
>
> . . . *Das Lied* carries this dimension of tonal language to its logical and inevitable conclusion, so that the final cadence at the end of Part II employs a full representation of the double-tonic complex, the chord of A-C-E-G, a combination sonority of the A minor

and C major triads. To describe this sonority as a major triad with added sixth is perfectly correct, but limited; for we must bear in mind that, since the function of this sonority is to bring A and C together, its arrangement as a kind of seventh chord is equally viable.20

The two elements of the double-tonic complex may be exposed in any one of a number of ways:

1. Juxtaposition of musical fragments implying the two tonics in succession or alternation.
2. Mixture of the two tonalities, exploiting ambiguous and common harmonic functions.
3. Use of a tonic sonority created by conflation of the two tonic triads.
4. Superposition of lines or textures in one key upon those in another.
5. Some combination of the above.

Each of these techniques is used at one time or another in Mahler's Ninth; only the third requires a brief additional comment at this point. The tonic sonority created by conflation of two triads is normally a tetrad, taking the form either of a triad with added seventh (example 1.1a) or of a triad with added sixth (example 1.1b). Use of a less compatible pair of modes creates a more complex sonority, and a clearer sense of the identity of each of the two tonics (examples 1.1c and d).

Example 1.1. Double-Tonic Sonorities

Just as in common practice not every triad functions as tonic, so in this music not every seventh or added-sixth chord represents a double tonic; the function is of course determined by context. It is interesting to note that Schenker, in one of his earliest publications (1906), expressed a not uncommon—but most un-Schenkerian—theory of the seventh chord: "Every seventh chord basically represents a conflict between two triads, from which conflict, however, only one triad can emerge as victor and, eventually, as peace-maker."[21] As Schenker delved more deeply into common-practice syntax, he developed the view that the seventh is generated by passing motion.[22] But since all surface characteristics of the common practice are retained in post-Wagnerian tonality, seventh chords (and other sonorities) may be generated either by linear motion, or by invocation of the double tonic; nor is it impossible for a given sonority to have *both* meanings.

Both Proctor and Bailey take it as axiomatic that later nineteenth-century chromaticism is structural rather than decorative. Proctor says that the chromatic scale substitutes for the diatonic scale as the source of tonal material.

> Diatonic material is then construed to be a special derivative of this underlying chromatic scale, and insofar as diatonic matter is present, the classical procedures for its manipulation are carried through into the new system. But the concept of the underlying chromatic scale opens up new structural possibilities, which . . . eventually work to undermine the specific qualities of tonal directedness peculiar to classical tonality.23

Bailey states that Mahler's tonal language

> . . . works around the pairing of tonalities, or, perhaps more accurately expressed, two chromatic modes . . . since each one has complete equivalence and interchangeability of major and minor. This consistent "modal mixture" makes it quite meaningless to attempt specifications of mode for large-scale units of a piece from this period, let alone whole movements. The illusion that a passage is in one mode or the other is barely more than that: an illusion created by a willful restriction of the *tonic triad* to one mode or the other.24

In a diatonic scale, there is only one upper third or one lower third normally available as a secondary structural degree to the principal tonic. But since the music with which we are concerned here is founded upon the chromatic scale, every tonic is flanked by *two* upper and *two* lower thirds, so that four complexes involving that principal tonic, and four secondary tonalities equally closely related to it, are available (see example 1.2).

Example 1.2. Chromatic Third Relationships

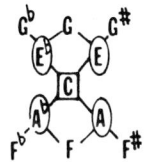

In a tertial complex, tonics a third apart are very closely related, and they may even substitute for each other under the right circumstances. Tonal progression by successive thirds is natural to the system, and structures may therefore be formed without that motion to the dominant which is essential in common practice. For example, progression from the upper *major* third of the principal tonic may be made either to the dominant (functioning as III of III) or to the minor sixth (augmented fifth), and from the upper *minor* third either to the dominant (III of III) or to the diminished fifth. In any of these cases, the succession of thirds may be extended, producing either an asymmetrical or a symmetrical subdivision of the octave. The symmetrical division will be by three major thirds or four minor thirds.[25] The close and distant relationships of classical tonality no longer apply; the key a tritone removed is as close a relative as the dominant — both are distant by two thirds. Proctor, describing symmetrical subdivisions of the octave, reaches a corollary conclusion:

> ... structural uses of the tritone can be frequent in chromatic tonality while they are virtually non-existent in classical tonality, where either or both of the boundaries of the tritone interval can only be found as part of an unstable linear complex. In chromatic [i.e., post-Wagnerian] tonality, tritone demarcators may be relatively stable points of division of the octave.[26]

This does not mean, however, that all common-practice characteristics disappear from music in the latter half of the nineteenth century. On the contrary, as Proctor puts it, "All of the operations of the classical system are retained in the body of techniques."[27] This compounds the problems of the analyst, who is thus enticed "to apply as much as he can of the classical tonal system, no matter how tenuous the connection between some classical device and a similar-appearing chromatic device might be."[28] These enticements of apparent conventionality must not lull the analyst into forgetting that structures predicated upon the double-tonic complex depend upon a Schenkerian structural dominant frequently at the foreground, occasionally at the middleground, and only rarely — in the classical sense — at the background. The "background" of such a piece is therefore not a unique contrapuntal structure common to all pieces in the style, and related by strict rules of voice-leading to the higher (more-to-the-foreground) levels, but a non-linear harmonic and tonal idea.[29] In the case of the Mahler symphonies, that idea always has to do with paired tonics.

Mahler's last completed symphonic work, the Ninth Symphony, is a highly developed representative of the post-Wagnerian tonal language. At the same time, it is a work which in many senses marks the end of the long Germanic symphonic tradition, but which can not be considered an anachronism in the decade which saw Schoenberg's own language evolve from that of *Verklärte Nacht* to *Das Buch der hängenden Gärten*. One of the fascinations of Mahler's late works is that they provide the groundwork from which Schoenberg and his disciples developed so much of the musical language of the twentieth century.

The earliest sketches for the Ninth apparently date from the summer of 1908, while Mahler was still in the midst of composing *Das Lied von der Erde*.[30] In the winter of 1908-09, he followed his usual practice of revising and orchestrating the composition of the previous summer, and then embarked upon the draft of the Ninth in the summer of 1909.[31] The scanty published sources are not entirely clear about the next two years. Alma writes of that summer (1909): "He had been working at full pressure and had finished the Ninth, but without venturing to call it so."[32] This *seems* to refer to *Das Lied*, the "real" Ninth Symphony, which, according to Alma, was not so called because of Mahler's superstition.[33] It is evident from other sources, however, that Alma did indeed mean the Ninth, and that Mahler, working at a terrific pace, was orchestrating the Finale by August.[34] In the autumn of 1909, Bruno Walter was shown a score of the Ninth in "almost illegible condition," just before Mahler took it to New York to "make a fair copy of it."[35] The haste with which the work had been composed gave rise to certain problems, and when Mahler turned again to his draft score, he found it necessary to make extensive revisions, especially to the second movement. This revised orchestral score (Walter's "fair copy") was started sometime after December 1909[36] and completed by April.[37] The following winter, the revised orchestral score was then copied by two New York copyists,[38] whose work, partly corrected by Mahler, became the *Stichvorlage*.[39]

The revisions were not completed, of course, because Mahler, who suffered from a weak heart diagnosed in 1907 and from intermittent severe inflammations of the throat, became seriously ill towards the end of February 1911. The disease developed into streptococcal infection of the blood, from which he died in Vienna on 18 May 1911.

The ill health of Mahler's final four years did not diminish his intellect. On the contrary, each of the last three works—*Das Lied*, the Ninth, and the unfinished Tenth—is a highly original expression of his creative powers. H. G. Wells remarks in his autobiography that "urgency for coherence and consistency, repugnance from haphazard assumptions and arbitrary statements . . . is the essential distinction of the educated and the uneducated mind."[40] If an analysis is to be more than a verbal description of a musical event, the analyst must assume that coherence and consistency are essential characteristics of a work of art—the ultimate means of expression of an educated mind—and that one of his principal tasks is to reveal their presence and character in a specific piece.

The integrity of the tonal world of Mahler's Ninth Symphony is to a great extent self-defined. As is usual in the music of this period, the tonal plot involves a "whole complex of interconnected keys" in contextually determined relationships, the tonal coherence of which is established by cross-referencing these keys at a number of levels.[41] A detailed analysis of each of the four movements shows how the formal design is always supported by a logical and consistent tonal plan. That plan is in each case dependent in some way upon exploitation of the relevant double-tonic complex. In particular, the constellations of third-related complexes which unfold throughout the first movement, and then generate the crucial material of the last three, derive ultimately from the opening complex of the work.

Example 1.3 shows the broad design of the whole symphony. The

Example 1.3. Design of the Ninth Symphony

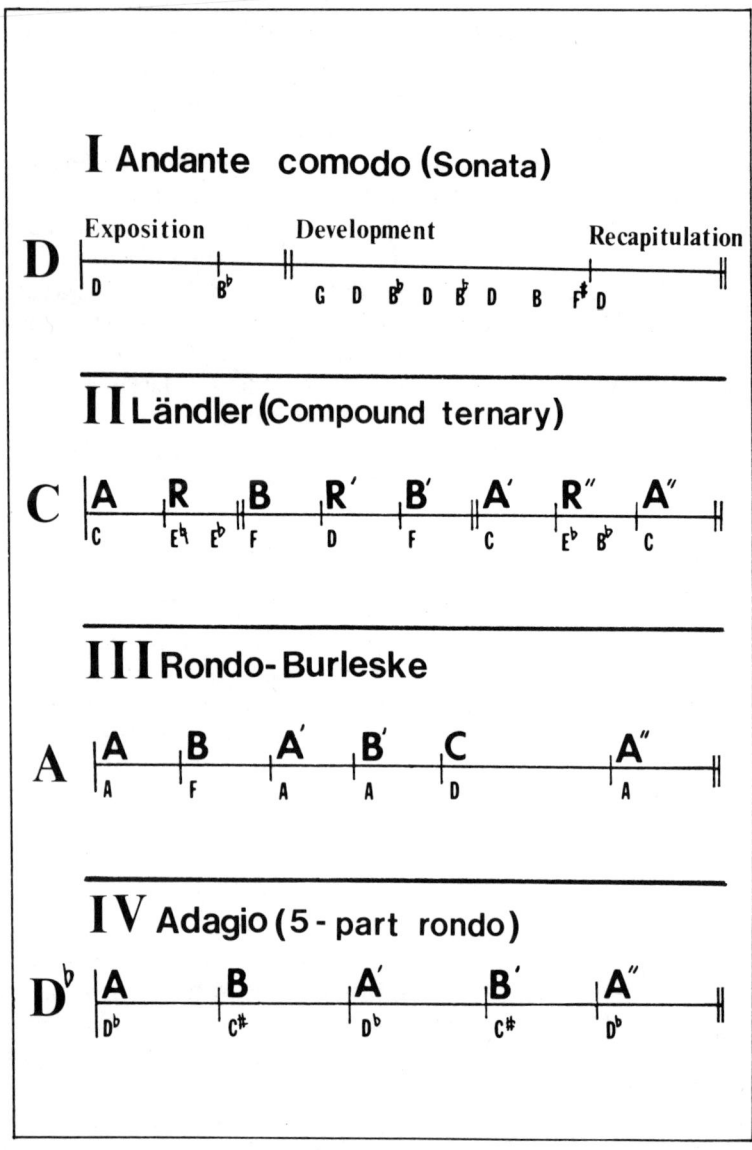

apparent conventionality of the four-movement plan is deceptive, for Mahler adopts the unique scheme of flanking two Scherzos with two slow movements. Further, each of the movements exhibits certain peculiarities of design or of tonal plan which raise provocative questions.

The *Andante Comodo* has been variously described as a sonata form, as a sonata combined with rondo, and as a sonata combined with rondo, variation *and* strophic song!⁴² The difficulties arise from the appearance of a "second theme" (at m. 27) in the tonic minor key (this theme is melodically identical with the theme of the second tonal area (m. 81)), and from the recurrence of the first theme in the tonic throughout the Development. What is the function of the D-minor episode at m. 27? Which of the many recurrences of the tonic signals the Recapitulation? And since the principal tonal areas are related by major thirds, to what extent does this plan manifest itself at other levels and in other movements?

The first Scherzo (so called originally; later "Menuetto infinito;" finally "*Ländler*"),⁴³ although curiously asymmetrical, is both structurally and harmonically the least complex movement; but paradoxically it was this movement with which Mahler had most difficulty. The Draft Score is itself evidence of continual changes: three substantial passages are stricken, one long insert is added, and numerous changes are made to individual passages. Even these alterations were not sufficient, and Mahler made important further revisions when he wrote the final full score. A comparison of the two versions will show how Mahler conceived the form of the movement and why he found it necessary to rework his original design.

The second Scherzo, *Rondo-Burleske*, violates the thematic and tonal principles of Rondo form. Furthermore, the dissonant linear counterpoint which comprises the greater part of the movement combines with double-tonic textures to produce a multiplicity of tonal ambiguities. But to understand the tonal framework which underlies the highly involved surface is to understand that the movement is a crucial link between the apparently disparate slow movements.

Considered as a self-contained movement, the *Adagio* is quite straightforward, but as the finale of this symphony, it poses certain problems. Why is there such a considerable motivic derivation from earlier movements? Why is there no prolonged tonal contrast in the entire movement? Is the symphony really in D, and for reasons unknown "happens to end, most poetically and appropriately, a semi-tone *below* the main tonic"?⁴⁴

The Finale of Mahler's Ninth is indeed both poetic and appropriate, but as part of the supreme achievement of an educated mind, it is also a coherent intellectual expression. Each of its apparent anomalies—and most especially the expressive falling semitone from the key of the first movement to that of the fourth—is consistent with, even a result of, the design of the symphonic whole.

2

Andante Comodo

Mahler's design for the first movement of the Ninth Symphony differs from the common-practice sonata form. That earlier model is a structure dependent upon the polarization of two key areas articulated in such a way that a large-scale structural dissonance occurs.[1] In classical sonata movements, the prolonged dominant which is the goal of the Development — and which is most often the key of the Second Tonal Area — is essential in two respects: it prolongs the tonic in creating the Schenkerian "fundamental structure," and it supports the "dissonant" second section which needs to be resolved as a whole. Post-Wagnerian tonal language, however, is not necessarily predicated upon the Schenkerian *Ursatz*, and therefore allows the tonal goal of

Example 2.1. Design of the *Andante comodo*

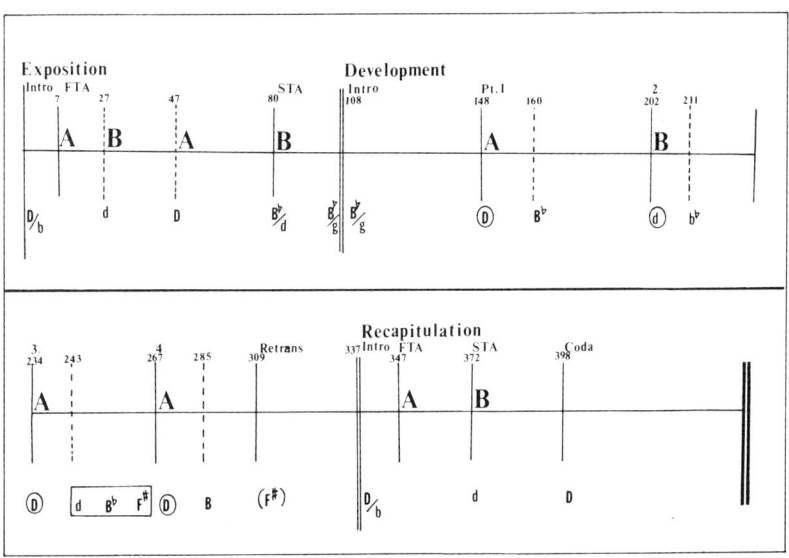

14 Andante Comodo

the development to be other than the dominant. If the sonata design is to remain coherent, then the musical structure must be predicated upon some tonal design which will allow for the sense of conflict and resolution essential to the dramatic idea of the sonata.

By overlaying implicitly and explicitly conflicting triads, Mahler establishes at the beginning of the Ninth Symphony a tonal world derived from a double-tonic complex of D and B. Rather than articulate a linear contrast of tonic and dominant, the Exposition unfolds the framework of a set of tertially connected principal and secondary keys. The Development does not prolong, but avoids the dominant, while working out the full delineation of the tonal plot initiated by the Exposition. Not until the requirements of this plot have been satisfied can any of the refrain-like returns of the tonic key be interpreted as recapitulatory (see example 2.1).

The movement begins with a six-measure introduction over a dominant pedal. This pedal does not, however, support a dominant triad. The functions of the introduction are to establish the primary tonality of D, to begin the process of setting B against D as the dissonant second element of the complex, and to introduce two motives which will be of crucial importance in articulating the tonal design and, therefore, the structure of the movement.

Example 2.2. S.S. and Sketch, mm. 1–7

Copyright 1912 by Universal Edition A.G. Copyright renewed. © Copyright 1969 Universal Edition A.G., Universal Edition, London. All rights reserved. Used by permission of European American Music Distributors Corporation, agent for Universal Edition.

At m. 3, the D-major triad is implied by motive "X" and then confirmed by the rising fourth (A-D) at the beginning of the horn entry (see example 2.2).[2] Here the B in motive "X" can be understood as a simple neighboring decoration, but motive "Y," by the sequential rising fourth from F-sharp to a metrically accented and sustained B, intensifies the significance of that note and begins to establish it as a point of secondary stability. As Peter Andraschke has observed,[3] "Y" is an elaboration of "X"; the B of m. 5 therefore still functions harmonically as a neighbor dissonance against the pedal A. In terms of the horn line alone, however, the B is consonant (stable): it is the goal of the passing C-sharp, and its rhythmic treatment ensures that melodically the A is heard as a neighboring decoration of B. That is, B has displaced A as the stable tone in this register, even though it is dissonant at a deeper level against the pedal note. The B-A displacement implies that the pitches D and F-sharp may be members of a D-major triad, or of a B-minor triad, or of both simultaneously; all are implicit in "X," and therefore also in its elaboration, "Y" (see example 2.3).

Example 2.3. Tonal Implication of Motive "X"

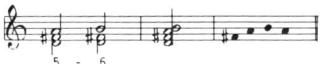

The resolution of the dominant pedal at m. 7 signifies the beginning of the First Tonal Area (FTA) proper. A number of commentators have shown in detail how the thematic material of the section is related to that of the introduction.[4] But we are concerned here primarily with the development of the tonal plot, and from this point of view, the FTA is designed to fulfill a number of functions:

1. Further to reinforce the principal tonality of D.
2. To develop the other side of the complex, so that B, which in the introduction serves as a melodic displacement, begins more clearly to support an opposing harmony.
3. To establish the legitimacy of either mode of D as tonic.
4. As a necessary concomitant of the prevailing duality of mode, to establish that B and B-flat assume equivalent functions in relation to D, and are therefore interchangeable at some levels.

The tonic sense is established by structuring the section around a series of prolongations of the D tonic triad which may be summarized as shown in example 2.4. At this level, the music is conventionally founded upon a prolongation of the tonic by the dominant; the whole passage may even be understood as a prolonged $\hat{3}$ followed by descent to $\hat{1}$. However, examination of the details makes it quite clear that the real significance of the

Example 2.4. Sketch of mm. 7-54

16 Andante Comodo

Example 2.5. Sketch of mm. 7-14

passage is its treatment of the ever-emerging D/B duality. The melodic line is developed from motivic references to the B-A displacement, and that motive also controls the melodic contour at a deeper level (see example 2.5). Mm. 9-12 prolong the B as a displacing neighbor to A, harmonized by the B in the doublebasses, which therefore acts as a disjunct neighbor, just as it did in the horn at m. 5. Thus the B is now treated in the melody as consonant neighbor (at the foreground) to A—a development of its role in the introduction—and in the bass as a tone supporting a harmony subsidiary to the tonic. The displacement or substitute function is reinforced at the points (marked by asterisks in example 2.5) where the neighbor stands in place of, or simultaneously with, its resolution.

The second phrase of the period (mm. 18-26) also prolongs D major; the B is again treated as a linear dissonance, both in the melodic line—a variant of that of the previous phrase—and by the inner-voice insistence on motive "X."

Motive "X" is so crucial that it is used to effect the change of mode as well: the neighbor B becomes B-flat in m. 26 (a change foreshadowed at m. 13), and the following period continues in D minor, with further exploitation of the B-flat/A displacement at several levels. Although constructed of already established motivic materials, the contour of the melody of this second period (mm. 27-36) differs from the first to such a degree that some commentators, ignoring the tonal plan, have referred to it as "Theme 2."[5] However, the background is founded upon an A/B-flat/A neighbor motion—in effect an elaboration of motive "X" in augmentation similar to that of the first period (see example 2.6). Note that at both m. 33 and m. 36, the neighbor function of the B-flat, although disguised by the disjunct compound line, is made clear by the carefully placed entries of D in the double bass; this is true as well of the inner-voice B-flat in the violoncello at m. 32, which must also be understood as a displacement of A.

The passage from mm. 39-46, the second phrase of this period, is

Example 2.6. Sketch of mm. 29-36

notable chiefly for being in the chromatic mode of D, combining all the crucial elements of D major and D minor in such a way that neither mode may be said to predominate. Since the function of a tonic is here not dependent upon a particular mode, either of the scale or of the tonic triad, change of mode must be regarded as a surface event not having anything like the structural force of an actual change of tonic.

Mm. 47–54, the third section of the FTA, also constitute a prolongation of D major, effected, as in mm. 7–25, by upper neighbor decoration of A in motive "X" (middle strings, harp and clarinet), a disjunct neighbor movement D-B-D in the bass line (doublebass), a background neighbor A-B-A in the principal melodic line (violin II), and, as an additional element, a prominent entry of motive "Y" in mm. 49–50 (violin I, trumpet). The whole is an extremely tightly-knit interweaving of melodic and harmonic threads of D major and B minor. Although D is certainly the principal tonic of the opening fifty-three measures, we see that its lower third is always present, linked to it, and necessary for its full realization. Further, the second period of the section establishes the legitimacy of D in either mode, and consequently the use of either of its lower thirds as the secondary member of the complex.

The interchangeability of mode is exploited at mm. 53 and 54; all voices resolve normally except that F-sharp becomes F-natural, and the dominant A is displaced by its upper neighbor B-flat. In harmonic terms, V of D resolves directly to I of B-flat. This signals the beginning of the Transition, the function of which is to prepare for the Second Tonal Area (STA) by effecting, or preparing, a reversal of the tonic complex relationship of the FTA. It will do this first by treating the secondary element as a key center, after which it becomes the principal element of its own double-tonic complex. In this case, the contrast is further emphasized by use of the minor form of the complex, already prepared in mm. 25–27.

For the first time, the secondary member of the original complex is tonicized; that is, it is made the subject of a foreground prolongation involving its own dominant (see example 2.7).

It is typical of Mahler's harmonic style that the dominant of the new key is not used to effect the modulation, which is instead accomplished by direct resolution from a chord of primary function in the departure key to one in the arrival key; the dominant is used only in a more local function, to prolong the new tonic. Note that all the modulations in the Exposition are

Example 2.7. Sketch of mm. 53–64

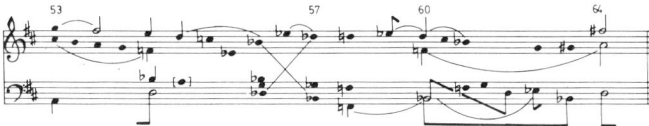

Andante Comodo

treated in this manner (see mm. 53–54, 63–64 and 77–80), as is the most crucial modulation in the whole movement, that which leads to the Recapitulation in m. 337.

Having established a key area of B-flat, the Transition then returns to the original complex, which is prolonged from m. 64 to m. 77. At m. 78, the mode of the complex is altered, and at m. 80, where the Second Tonal Area begins, the polarity of the complex is reversed. The role of the lower third degree has been carefully developed with this end in view. At the beginning, B appears, almost incidentally, implied by the linear neighbor movement, superimposed upon a strong D-major triad; then the sense of two triads is more fully developed (mm. 7–26) as B is used in the melody on several levels; at the same time, the bass line establishes the first harmonic movement, a progression from D to B, and for the first time B supports a harmony in opposition to D; finally, from mm. 54–63, the B-flat in opposition to D; finally, from mm. 54–63, the B-flat is given triadic representation and prolonged, and thus the vertical conflict present from the beginning of the work becomes a "linear," or structural dissonance in Rosen's terms.

The STA must do more than simply present a single key in dissonance against that of the FTA, since the piece has from the first been concerned with *dual* tonalities. This section therefore must not only establish some tonal contrast with the preceding material, but must also prepare for the tonal complexity of the Development section, and for the eventual Recapitulation. The first of these goals is achieved by reversal of the polarities of the original double-tonic complex, so that B-flat is heard as the principal key, with D as a "dissonant" overlay, and the second by inversion of the complex of thirds around B-flat, so that the secondary key will be the lower, rather than the upper third. As we shall see, the *two* lower thirds of B-flat are crucial in framing the Development section, and one of them serves as a tertial link to the Recapitulation.

Example 2.8 shows the cadence of the Transition and the opening measures of the STA. As we noted above, the dominant of the new key appears only after the tonic is established—that is, at m. 83. But the preced-

Example 2.8. S.S., mm. 76–83

Copyright 1912 by Universal Edition A.G. Copyright renewed. © Copyright 1969 Universal Edition A.G., Universal Edition, London. All rights reserved. Used by permission of European American Music Distributors Corporation, agent for Universal Edition.

ing measures present an involved set of tonal implications. The C-sharp in the horns at m. 79, later picked up by the harp, 'cello and flute, is heard in three different harmonic contexts, and it is the ambiguity of these multiple meanings which provides the "common area" of the modulation. First, of course, C-sharp functions as the leading tone of the cadential key, D. This influence is so strong that for the next three measures, with the exception of the bass line, the music is far more easily understood in D than in B-flat (see example 2.9). The conflict of the D/B-flat association is not only carried over into the STA, but actually intensified; only now, it is elements of D which are in dissonant relation to B-flat as the fundamental key. This melodic material occurs directly stated three more times (at mm. 90, 211 and 372). Each time the passage is harmonized differently, and each time the D/B-flat duality emerges, but only at the last occurrence, in the Recapitulation, is the conflict resolved.

Example 2.9. S.S., mm. 79-81

Copyright 1912 by Universal Edition A.G. Copyright renewed. © Copyright 1969 Universal Edition A.G., Universal Edition, London. All rights reserved. Used by permission of European American Music Distributors Corporation, agent for Universal Edition.

The C-sharp of mm. 79-80 must also be considered in relation to the primary tonality, B-flat, which is established by the B-flat/F oscillation in the basses and the aspects of the texture common to both B-flat and D. The horn figure derives motivically from the A-B neighbor of the introduction and resolves as a chromatic neighbor in all parts except violin I; here one must consider that there is a transfer of the resolution to the trumpet, whose figure is a development of the original horn motive (see example 2.10).

Example 2.10. S.S., mm. 80-82

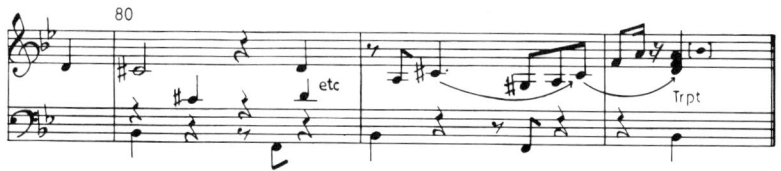

Copyright 1912 by Universal Edition A.G. Copyright renewed. © Copyright 1969 Universal Edition A.G., Universal Edition, London. All rights reserved. Used by permission of European American Music Distributors Corporation, agent for Universal Edition.

20   Andante Comodo

There is still another way of hearing this C-sharp and that is as D-flat, the third degree of B-flat *minor*. We have already discussed the alternation and mixture of parallel major and minor in connection with the FTA. The same device is used in B-flat, almost from the first moment of its appearance as a key center. In particular, there is juxtaposition of major and minor thirds (mm. 55 and 56) and of the major and minor sixth degrees (lower thirds) of the scale mm. 56–57 and 58–59). This prepares both versions of the B-flat complex: the complex of B-flat and G and that of B-flat and G-flat. We shall see below how this implication is more fully explored at m. 211 ff.

All interpretations of the C-sharp are certainly heard in the context of a fundamental tonality of B-flat. In the broadest view, all of mm. 80–96 comprise a I-V-I progression in B-flat, with a prolongation of the V from m. 83 to m. 95 (see example 2.11). Two important features should be noted. First, at m. 90, there is a powerful return of the melodic material from mm. 80 ff. In this first attempt to resolve the ambiguities inherent in the original presentation, the implication of D is more fully realized. While B is present, it is clearly treated as a passing tone down to A. However, the C-sharp in the horns (and elsewhere), while a crucial member of the temporary key (D), occurs as an unresolved dissonant element. Further, the V-I progression in D functions here, for the first time in the piece, simply as the first interval in a chain of fifths leading to B-flat, and therefore as an agent prolonging B-flat, and not itself part of the fundamental harmony being prolonged.

Example 2.11.   Sketch of mm. 80–96

This brings us to the second point to be noted in the passage, concerning the lower third degree which now supersedes D as the secondary member of the complex. It is significant that this new element first occurs immediately after the disappearance of the last superimposed D (m. 82). At m. 83, the crucial motive designated "Y" in example 2.2 recurs, but transposed so that the tonal implications are of B-flat and—fleetingly—G. Now, just as alternate modes of D were used in the FTA to establish the legitimacy of either B or B-flat as the lower third to D, so B-flat minor is introduced here to allow G-flat as an alternative to G. The point is made perfectly clear by the appearance of G-flat in a minor mode statement of motive "Y" at mm. 100–101 (see example 2.12). What follows reinforces the connection

Example 2.12. Motive "Y"

by having bass resolutions of V-I with first a suspended G-flat, and then, in the final cadential resolution of the Exposition, sustention of the tonic triad with a strongly emphasized superimposition of the "added sixth," G-natural.

Although motive "Y" occurs only four times in the course of the Exposition, an understanding of its role in elucidating the tonal progress of the section explains why Mahler found it impossible to allow the introduction to stand in its original form, without this figure.[6] In the altered version of the Draft Score, "Y" appears in four crucial places: at the first suggestion of the D/B complex (mm. 3-4), at the last presentation of that complex (mm. 49-50), at the first presentation of the second complex (mm. 83-84), and at the statement of the minor form of that complex (mm. 100-101).

Example 2.13. Tonal Plot of the Exposition

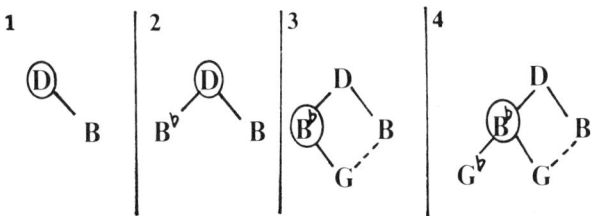

The unfolding of the tertial complexes of the tonal plot in the Exposition may be summarized in four stages (see example 2.13). The circle indicates the principal *tonic* of the complex. By the end of the Exposition, only D and B-flat have been fully realized as fundamental key centers. If the train of tonal thought thus suggested is to proceed consistently, there will appear full-fledged tonicizations of the remaining tonics (B, G-flat and G), possible introduction and tonicization of E-flat (the common lower third of G-flat and G), and eventual arrival at D from G-flat (F-sharp). Note that at the third stage the G, while introduced as the lower third of B-flat, may also function as the lower third of B, an as-yet-unrealized connection indicated by the broken line. The continuation of the chain of circumstances initiated in the Exposition is illustrated in example 2.14, which shows two lines of progress: a principal line arpeggiating through major thirds with a similar secondary line formed from the lower thirds associated with the first set.

It is precisely with these tonal areas, and *only* these areas, that the Development is concerned. The classical development section, on the other

Example 2.14. Tonal Plot of the First Movement

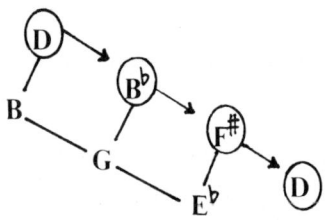

hand, was normally structured around a *single* fundamental tonal idea — the prolongation of the dominant. The entry of the tonic key at the point of recapitulation must be understood not as a resolution of that dominant, but as a recommencement following interruption.[7] Thus it is necessary to have again, near the end of the movement, a structural dominant which this time *will* resolve. But the development section of the Mahler IX most certainly does not prolong the dominant. As we shall see below, the only dominant sonorities in the section must be interpreted as having only local functions. There is no apparent sequential, linear or functional approach in the common-practice sense to the final harmony of the Development section.

Mahler's Development is an extension not just of the STA, but of the entire Exposition. It does not simply progress from B-flat to F-sharp, but continues to work out in alternation the tonal plot of the D/B complex and its further implications.

A common-practice development is incomplete until the V *Stufe* has been reached and made unstable (established as V of I rather than I of V); thereafter, a return of the FTA key — usually articulated by FTA melodic material — signals the beginning of the recapitulation. Here, however, the Development will be incomplete until G, E-flat and B have been tonicized, and F-sharp reached and made unstable. No occurrence of FTA key or melodic material may be interpreted as recapitulatory until these conditions have been satisfied. Thus, the rondo-like returns of D-major throughout this section are explicable in the technical sense, and are not anomalies in the sonata-form structure of the movement.

There is as well a poetic explanation for these sections, consistent with Mahler's compositional world. It has been suggested that the structure of the movement combines elements of *Lied* with those of sonata form.[8] It seems clear that the *Lied* element involved here is the refrain, represented by recurrences of the FTA material and principal key.

In refrain structures — the *formes fixes*, simple ternary, Baroque concerto, song with refrain — identical or very similar sections frequently must serve different roles in the structure. One may find identical introductory, bridging and concluding refrains. The effect is perhaps most clearly seen in a literary structure such as Dylan Thomas's "Do not go gentle into that good night," in which a recurrent line derives its meaning and even its syntactical function from the context in which it is found.

In Mahler's development section, too, the refrain is significant not so much for itself as for its context, for in each case the D major (or minor) is preparation for further exploration of the tonic complex and its ancillary keys; each refrain is succeeded by a new aspect of the unfolding tonal plot. Example 2.15 illustrates the resulting structure: four refrains, each followed by a developmental episode, with the whole framed by an introductory episode and retransition.

Example 2.15. Design of the Development

Intro.	1		2		3		4		Retrans.
	R.	Ep.	R.	Ep.	R.	Ep.	R.	Ep.	
B♭ G	D	B♭ E♭ G	D	B♭ min.	D	D B♭ F♯	D	B maj.	F♯

Because the relationship between the refrain and the following episode becomes each time more tonally remote, the transitions between refrain and episode become more complex, and the tonal structure of the refrains becomes each time more closed. The process culminates in the Recapitulation, which is in effect the last refrain and is therefore harmonically fully closed. This view of the Recapitulation as one more refrain is further supported by Mahler's careful foreshadowing of the Retransition preceding the last refrain of the Development. The following discussion will deal first with the refrain sections and then with the episodes that provide the true development.

The first refrain-episode pair of the Development is structured broadly as a microcosm of the Exposition; the refrain itself is similar in design to the onset of the FTA: mm. 142–47 constitute an introduction over a sustained pedal, followed by a return of the first theme in D major. The occurrence of D major, however, is merely transitory and leads to the episode in B-flat.

The transition to the refrain exemplifies again a modulatory process typical of Mahler's style. It is the exception, rather than the rule, for modulation to be accomplished by progression, either diatonic or chromatic, to the dominant of the key. Rather, resolution is made directly to the new tonic from either the dominant or, often, the tonic of the old key.

From G minor at m. 130, normal progression leads to B-flat (a reversal, as we shall see below, of the motion that opens the Development, thus again referring to the B-flat/G connection which closed the Exposition). B-

24 Andante Comodo

Example 2.16. S.S., mm. 130–35

Copyright 1912 by Universal Edition A.G. Copyright renewed. © Copyright 1969 Universal Edition A.G., Universal Edition, London. All rights reserved. Used by permission of European American Music Distributors Corporation, agent for Universal Edition.

flat is immediately made unstable by the introduction of E-natural, so that the B-flat triad is now heard as IV of F. But the crucial move from the B-flat triad to D minor is made in such a way that the note B-flat is treated as a displacement of A (see example 2.16).

The D-major refrain segment (mm. 148–59) consists of nothing more than tonic and dominant harmonies, but is designed so that the dominant is never permitted to have a full structural resolution. Its function is always to effect a *local* prolongation, or, by interruption, to avoid the structural resolution. The section consists of three melodically similar four-measure phrases, the first two of which terminate with interruption. The note D in the first violin at m. 151 does not represent the resolution of the preceding scale degree $\hat{2}$, nor does the D-major chord which supports it resolve the preceding dominant. The entire measure is heard as dominant, with the third-beat tonic subsidiary to that function; and since the fundamental line recommences at m. 152 (with higher-octave displacement), the resolution of the dominant function is interrupted. At the corresponding point in phrase two (m. 155), the same thing happens melodically, but with a simpler treatment of the dominant (see example 2.17).

Example 2.17. Sketch of mm. 148–60

The common-practice expectation is for the third phrase again to establish the dominant, but then allow it to initiate closure for both the harmony and the melodic line. However, the function of this section is not to establish D major, but to lead to some other key in opposition to D, and the dominant of mm. 158–59 resolves directly to the tonic of B-flat. The subtlety of this resolution is noteworthy, for both the bass line and the upper voice resolve as they would in D; the $\hat{3}$-$\hat{2}$-$\hat{1}$ line is transferred at m. 158 to the bassoons and completes itself in a conveniently sparse texture at m. 160. But the inner-voice alteration of F-sharp to F-natural, and the substitution of B-flat for A provide the required harmonic diversion to the key of the episode.

The second refrain extends from m. 202 to m. 210. There is virtually no harmonic motion in the passage. It is approached by a direct change from B-flat (functioning as V/E-flat) to D minor, with C-sharp as a long delayed passing note (see example 2.18).

Example 2.18. Beginning of the Second Refrain

Thematically, the passage derives from the second period of the FTA. It now transpires that one of the reasons the melody of the second tonal area appears first as part of the FTA is so that it may recur in the Development, in D, and be perceived as a refrain. All nine measures are simply decoration of the D-minor triad over a continuous D pedal. The passage is made inherently unstable by the sustained C-sharp, passed at m. 204 from trombone to 'cello and then to the basses. There are foreground-level resolutions of this dissonance from m. 206 on, but the final resolution is withheld until m. 211. A discussion of that resolution appears below as a preliminary to the analysis of the episode it initiates.

The third and fourth refrains might be thought of as comprising a single large section, since there is no great sense of discontinuity, and since the intervening episodic material is only twenty measures long and is thematically sparse. Nonetheless, the similarity of the material of mm. 246–67 to that of the Retransition lets it be heard as an episode, while the following measures are a last developmental refrain. The third refrain, then, comprises an introductory three measures founded on a harmonic resolution of V-I supporting a melodic descent from $\hat{5}$ to $\hat{3}$, and a sustention of that degree through seven measures with inner-voice movement exploiting the 6-5 displacement that is one of the motivic germs of the whole movement (see example 2.19). The transition to Episode 4 is made through a "deceptive" resolution of the dominant which thereby avoids the expected *harmonic* closure apparently needed to support the $\hat{3}$-$\hat{2}$-$\hat{1}$ descent in the horns, and diverts the harmony from D to B-flat (see example 2.20).

Example 2.19. Sketch of mm. 234–37

Example 2.20. Transition to Episode 4

Example 2.21. Sketch of mm. 267–75

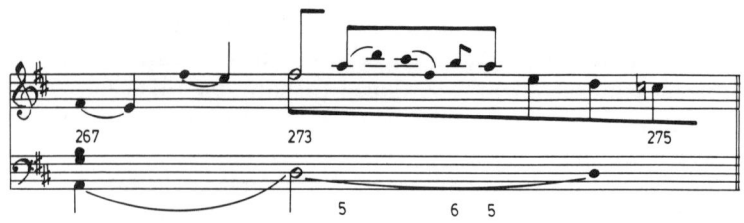

The last refrain is the shortest, but that which most fully incorporates all the principal melodic figures of the opening section of the FTA. In addition, it is the only refrain which is in any sense both melodically and harmonically closed, albeit with a closure which is almost immediately made unstable (see example 2.21). At mm. 273–75, the D triad, by the addition of C-natural, begins the modulation to B, the key of the last episode. But as this occurs, there is a prominent and significant return of motive "Y" (upper strings) for the first time since m. 49. This is the final reference before the Retransition to the original complex of linked and opposed keys, D and B. It occurs just as D is being affirmed by cadence for the first and last time in the Development, and just before the first tonicization of the other member of the complex, B — a tonicization which is the crucial point of the last section of the Development proper. We shall now examine the episodes that precede this culmination.

Andante Comodo 27

We have seen in some detail how the $\hat{6}$-$\hat{5}$ displacement generates both melodic and harmonic motives which in turn are realized on a larger scale to provide the essential tonal degrees of the Exposition. Thus, B (or B-flat) is used to color the D triad, or to provide the sound of D and B triads together, or to give B (flat) as an alternative to D locally—as at m. 54; and at a larger level, the secondary feature of the D/B complex becomes the primary tonal center of the STA. In a precisely analogous fashion, the sixth superimposed on the B-flat cadence at the end of the Exposition becomes the primary tonic in the following section.

Of course, there are always *two* lower thirds, and in the cadential approach reference has been made to both G and G-flat by important entries of motive "Y." The long, tonally unstable passage which follows the cadence of the Exposition exploits the connection of the G-minor and B-flat triads, and the use of both lower thirds to B-flat. Although the G is ultimately far more stable in this section than the G-flat, the strong B-flat/G-flat interval established in the first measures is a subtle foreshadowing of the powerful F-sharp of the other flanking section, the Retransition. More detailed reference to this connection will be made below. Indeed, mm. 108-14 establish a symmetrical structure around a sustained B-flat which summarizes the three most important tonal centers of the movement: D, B-flat and F-sharp (see example 2.22).

Example 2.22.   Sketch of mm. 108-19

Example 2.23.   Sketch of mm. 108-19

The temporary ambiguity of tonal center engendered by the augmented triad is quickly dispelled as both D and B-flat are treated as suspensions resolved by voice transferral (trombones at m. 114 to horns at m. 116, and horns at m. 115 to violas and 'cellos in m. 118). Henceforth, in this section, G-flat functions only as the leading tone to G. The passage may be summarized as shown in example 2.23.

In spite of the contrapuntal strength of the resolution to G minor, the close connection of this key with its principal, B-flat, is maintained. Twelve measures (mm. 119–30) subtly alternate between G minor and B-flat. The following passage (mm. 130–42) reverses the $\hat{6}$-$\hat{5}$'s which have led from D to B-flat to G and thus prepares for the return to D and the ensuing refrain. Example 2.24 shows how the G-minor triad is placed in a B-flat context by use of the neighbor F-natural, and then in G minor by use of F-sharp. At mm. 126–28, the two are overlapped; the strings are clearly in B-flat, with the brasses just as clearly in G minor. At m. 130, the resolution in all voices is to G minor, followed at once by a V-I resolution in B-flat, from whence, by the process described above, the tonal sequence is continued to D. In abstraction, the process is one of inversion to produce a 6/3 sonority, with resolution of the $\hat{6}$ down to $\hat{5}$ to reach the new triad a third away (see example 2.24b). The return to D major for the first refrain is thus accomplished by a linear realization at the foreground of the technique which provides the rationale of the tertially connected tonic complex, and which generates the tonal background of the Exposition.

Example 2.24. Reduction of mm. 119–23

The episode following the first refrain (mm. 160–201) is tonally the most complex. We have earlier observed that a realization of the logical framework hypothesized from analysis of the Exposition will require, among other things, tonicization of E-flat and G, and, in order to permit eventual movement towards the Recapitulation, a destabilization of B-flat. The three processes occur in this first episode and are accomplished by means of the 6-5 displacement.

The episode begins at m. 160 with a direct modulation into B-flat created by the flat-$\hat{6}$ substitution for $\hat{5}$ above D. In abstract terms, the section is designed around different chordal structures above this supporting bass note. The B-flat 6/3 acts as V of E-flat; the change of position is effected by a linear motion through a sixth in the bass. Note that while the E-flat triad of m. 166 is not truly tonicized until the V-I resolution of mm. 170–72, and the E-flat in the bass at mm. 165–66 serves merely a passing function, the upper strings are firmly in E-flat. The tonal significance of these few bars is shown also by the prominent return of thematic material derived from the melody of the first theme. Here, in fact, is the

Example 2.25. Sketch of mm. 160-82

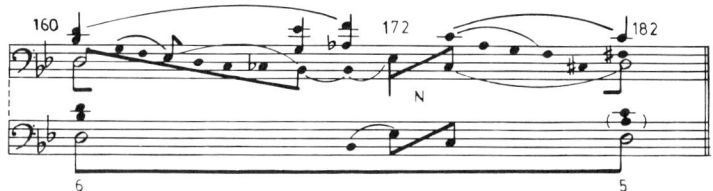

only occurrence in the movement of this particular material in a key other than D. The sixth-descent in the bass is exactly reversed at the cadence chord, and the point of arrival of the line (C) is strongly articulated by surface features, so that while C is not tonicized, its structural importance is made clear, and it can be understood as functioning with E-flat as part of a double neighbor around D (see example 2.25).

As example 2.25 shows, the bass note D is prolonged from m. 160 (and earlier) past m. 182, but at this latter point another $\hat{6}$-$\hat{5}$ motion occurs, producing again a D-major triad. There can be no question, however, of this being understood as a prolongation of the D-major tonic of the preceding refrain, since the upper-voice motion from m. 160 has been a step-descent from D to C. The sonority thus produced — the dominant seventh of G — is very simply prolonged by passing and neighboring motions (including a change of mode) until m. 195 (see example 2.26). At this point, G and B-flat are neighbors to F-sharp and A respectively, prolonging the D seventh chord, but Mahler *resolves* them as passing tones (harmonized by passing E and C-sharp) to V/E-flat. The treatment of the B-flat as a dominant counteracts the stability it had achieved by the end of the Exposition, and neither B-flat major nor either one of the two secondary keys of this episode is again established as a prolonged tonic triad; they have already been "developed," and therefore have played out their role in the tonal plot.

Episode 2, following a brief D-minor refrain, is concerned tonally with a single key, B-flat minor, and thematically with an attempt to reconcile the inherent conflicts of the theme of the STA. B-flat minor, although of course a legitimate version of the lower third key of D, is more distantly related to

Example 2.26. Sketch of mm. 182-98

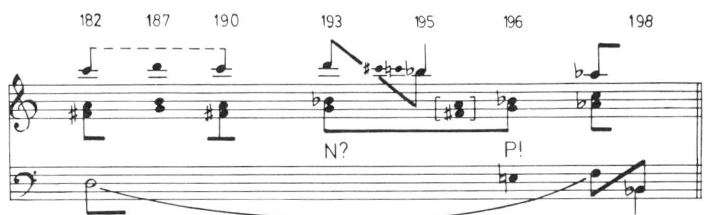

30 *Andante Comodo*

Example 2.27. Three Versions of the Second Theme

Copyright 1912 by Universal Edition A.G. Copyright renewed. © Copyright 1969 Universal Edition A.G., Universal Edition, London. All rights reserved. Used by permission of European American Music Distributors Corporation, agent for Universal Edition.

it than is B-flat major, and this section therefore offers a further development of the complex of the double tonic.

Example 2.27 shows the STA theme as it first occurred in the FTA, harmonized in D minor (mm. 29 ff.), as it occurred in the STA, harmonized in D/B-flat (mm. 81 ff.), and as it occurs in Episode 2, harmonized in B-flat minor. In example 2.27a, the A is stable, but C-sharp requires resolution; in example 2.27b, both A and C-sharp require resolution; in the third attempt, C-sharp is stable, but A requires resolution. Each of these versions of the theme therefore includes an inherent conflict between the harmonic implications of the melody and the actual harmonization. That these conflicts are crucial, and that their solution must be harmonic (tonal) rather than melodic is evident upon comparison of the three extracts, for every note *except* the first five may change to suit the harmonic context. M. 211 presents unresolved chromatic appoggiaturas against a stable triad, and this idea is so vital that it forms the basis for the foreground of much of the episode. It gives rise to the melodic alterations to E-natural and G-sharp in

Example 2.28. S.S., mm. 211–15

Copyright 1912 by Universal Edition A.G. Copyright renewed. © Copyright 1969 Universal Edition A.G., Universal Edition, London. All rights reserved. Used by permission of European American Music Distributors Corporation, agent for Universal Edition.

m. 212 which resolve at the end of m. 213, as well as to the inner voices of mm. 212-22 (see example 2.28).

Mm. 219-22 show a prolongational technique so typical of this movement as to be almost motivic. The bass line describes a direct, though partially chromatic descent through an octave from B-flat, but in such a way that it is not possible to construe the motion as an elaboration of an arpeggiation through the dominant. The impulse to the lower B-flat is a purely contrapuntal rather than a harmonic resolution. The uppermost voice *does* arpeggiate a triad, but it is the tonic; the A-natural reached in the violas in m. 221 and then picked up by the horns, violin I, violoncello and lower woodwinds is not fully resolved until m. 224. Note as well that the triple appoggiatura in the middle strings (m. 219) produces a strongly articulated G-flat minor 6/3 as a substitute for the primary B-flat minor triad, in the manner that is by now an expected, rather than a "deceptive" resolution (see example 2.29).

Example 2.29. Sketch of mm. 219-34

The transition to the third refrain again prolongs B-flat (minor) — for the last time in the movement — and again without any reference to a dominant. As example 2.29 shows, the essential technique is that of neighbor-passing subdominant in m. 227 (incidentally reversing the B-flat/E-flat relationship of the previous episode) approached by its own subdominant. After inversion of the tonic triad there occurs the only passage in the episode directed by functional progression. These measures (229-33) progress to a pre-dominant sonority in B-flat minor, but the definitive dominant, avoided throughout the episode, is replaced by the dominant of D major, which initiates the ensuing refrain.

The third episode (mm. 246-66) is unique in that it does not have a clearly defined beginning in a non-tonic key, but resembles the dependent transition of certain common-practice sonata movements, overlapping thematically and tonally with the preceding section. The immediate goal of the first phrase is G-flat; the tonal progression from D through B-flat to G-flat thus is a representation in miniature of the large-scale tonal movement from the FTA through the STA to the end of the Development, and in this way serves to foreshadow the Retransition. At the same time, by means of one-measure displacements in the horn, subtle reference is again made to the conflicts inherent in the theme of the STA (see example 2.30). Note that

32 *Andante Comodo*

Example 2.30. S.S., mm. 246–50

Copyright 1912 by Universal Edition A.G. Copyright renewed. © Copyright 1969 Universal Edition A.G., Universal Edition, London. All rights reserved. Used by permission of European American Music Distributors Corporation, agent for Universal Edition.

the horns in m. 247 imply the D-minor triad, resolving the double passing notes of the previous measure. The resolution is of course displaced from its normal coincidence with the D/A in the bass of m. 246. The violin fragment of m. 247 is therefore harmonized with two different triads, and the problematic A, C-sharp and F are all consonant with one or the other. Similarly, in m. 248, the displaced A/E in the horns harmonizes the violins' A, and the C-sharp is heard both as the third of the horns' incomplete triad and as a D-flat in conjunction with the bass strings. Therefore, the various interpretations of the melodic problems of the theme shown above in example 2.27 are recapitulated with the harmonic succession outlining the tonal cornerstones of the movement. The importance of the temporary goal of G-flat is emphasized by its sustention through four slow measures, lengthened by two fermatas. Further, this harmonic progression becomes the basis for much of the important detail in the succeeding three movements.

The second phrase of the episode is in a sense a reflection of the first: again the goal is G-flat (F-sharp), achieved by sequential connection of that triad with B-flat and D (see example 2.31). The opening E-flat minor triad functions as IV of B-flat (mm. 257–59); sequential repetition gives IV-I in D minor, and G-flat, which at first functions as IV of D-flat, itself becomes the goal at mm. 264–66. From this point, direct resolution is made to the dominant of D major for the following refrain.

Example 2.31. Reduction of mm. 253–66

Copyright 1912 by Universal Edition A.G. Copyright renewed. © Copyright 1969 Universal Edition A.G., Universal Edition, London. All rights reserved. Used by permission of European American Music Distributors Corporation, agent for Universal Edition.

Example 2.32. Sketch of mm. 277-85

The final episode is introduced by a brief transition (mm. 267-85) from its refrain. The tonal process bears a familial resemblance to that which began the Development by establishing the two lower thirds of B-flat and interpreting the lower of the two as the leading tone to the other. In this instance, the whole process occurs in conjunction with a bass ascent through a sixth, making a direct linear connection between the starting point D and the arrival at B (see example 2.32).

The episode is in two parts; each half ends with an F-sharp ninth chord which does not, however, fulfill the same function both times. In none of the preceding episodes is the music structured around the tonic-dominant relationship in any sense except for transitory resolutions at the most immediate level of the foreground. Here, however, following a typical prolongation of the tonic triad by inner-voice motion (mm. 285-89), there begins a complex harmonic motion, the goal of which is the powerfully articulated dominant of mm. 296-98 — a dominant which resolves to its tonic (in m. 299) and which is the only strong dominant in any episode to do so (see example 2.33).

Example 2.33. Sketch of mm. 285-99

The dissonant prolongation of D major encompassed by these measures is an important component of the overall prolongation of B. Highly significant is the way the third of the prolonged D major provides the root of the ensuing F-sharp chord. A reversal of this connection is used to effect the transition to the Recapitulation, foreshadowed at mm. 266-67. Thus there is a double irony in this half of the episode. Apparently the most stable of the episodes because of its strong dominant, it anticipates the ultimate instability of the Retransition; the F-sharp chord itself, seemingly significant for its local function as dominant, is really crucial since it will soon function *not* as dominant.

34   *Andante Comodo*

Example 2.34.   Sketch of mm. 299–310

Example 2.34 shows a sketch of the second half of this episode. Several similarities with the first part are immediately noticeable. In both parts, there is a brief prolongation of the tonic and a progression over an arpeggiated diminished triad to a B-flat seventh chord. But while the first B-flat moves directly to D, the second functions as a secondary dominant to the dominant of A-flat. Although this tonality is incidental to the main tonal plot and is not fully tonicized, the reference again demonstrates the ubiquity of the tertial relationship at middle-ground and deeper levels. The last appearance in the Development of the motive "Y" is at the beginning of this episode (mm. 286–87). An interpretation consistent with those made earlier requires that this motive imply B major and G-sharp. The excursion of mm. 302–7 is a deeper-level manifestation of this reference, and thus completes the tonal network. The work has explored the principal complex of D and its lower thirds, as well as the secondary complexes arising from those degrees. The tonal requirements of the Development are now almost satisfied. All that remains is the establishment of an unstable F-sharp. Therefore the resolution to F-sharp in m. 309 is very different from that of m. 298, since the later one is greatly extended so that it initiates and supports the whole of the Retransition.

The F-sharp pedal of the Retransition for much of the time supports ostinato recurrences of motive "X." Indeed, it now appears that this figure, from which the crucial tonal indicator "Y" is derived is itself transformed and used as a structural and tonal signpost throughout the movement.

The motive is, of course, related by transposition to the three-note cell which Robert Bailey has shown to control the tonal design of *Das Lied von der Erde*.[9] Not only the shape of the motive, but also the manner of its chromatic alteration demonstrate the creative continuity between Mahler's last two completed symphonic works. Example 2.35 shows that all other versions of the motive are derived by semi-tone alteration from the first form and similarly imply specific triadic backgrounds.

Version 1-i in example 2.35b and its simple rhythmic variants ii and iii occur only in refrain statements where their function is to imply D-major and B-minor triads. The figure is therefore a prominent feature of the FTA (in a sense, the first refrain), of the first and fourth refrains of the Development, and at the very beginning of the Recapitulation. Its appearance in a vitally significant altered form in the Coda will be discussed below.

Example 2.35. Variants of Motive "X"

Version 2 combines scalar elements of D major and D minor; it is used to connect the two sections of the FTA differentiated by mode. It is followed at once by versions 3-i and 3-ii which imply D minor and its associated lower third, B-flat. At m. 132, the variant 3-iii exploits these implications to provide the direct link in a modulation through B-flat to D minor.

Version 4-i appears at mm. 110 ff, and, with enharmonic respelling as 4-ii, at m. 124. It is the first version of the motive to be used in the Development, and it is the only derivitive which is inherently unstable—that is, not a possible indicator of a tonic-function sonority—because of the tritone between its extremes. The respelling at m. 124 is simply a notational convenience to allow the G-flat to function as leading tone to G. But the most interesting feature of 4-i is its relationship to 1-iv, and to the harmony implied by the first five measures of the Retransition.

Example 2.36. Motive "X" in the Retransition

When version 1 recurs at m. 317, it does so in such a way that the B *must* be construed as a non-chord element dissonant against the strongly articulated C in the lower brass. Thus, motive 1 here has a non-tonic function and is directly related to 4, with which the Development begins. The relationship is even clearer if the chordal implication of mm. 310-14 is considered (see example 2.36). At m. 310, the beginning of the Retransition, one hears the sonority which has a local function of V/B. At m. 314, the climactic moment of the whole Development, the fifth is lowered to bring back the sonority implied by m. 110. To make the connection unmistakable, the return is signalled by the recurrence—for the first time since the opening measures of the Development—of a powerful rhythmic figure:

36   *Andante Comodo*

♩. ♪ ♩. . While it would be wrong to suggest that the whole of the Development may be analytically reduced to represent a prolongation of this sonority, the manner of their articulation makes it certain that these two references to "X" are heard as similar poles marking the boundaries of the Development.

Example 2.37.   The Retransition

Copyright 1912 by Universal Edition A.G. Copyright renewed. © Copyright 1969 Universal Edition A.G., Universal Edition, London. All rights reserved. Used by permission of European American Music Distributors Corporation, agent for Universal Edition.

Example 2.37 is a reduction of the entire Retransition. The first eight measures prolong the dissonant function of the B and the non-tonic (unstable) implication of the F-sharp and A of motive "X," first by simple extension of the C natural, then by superimposition upon the ostinato motive of triads extracted from the dominant sonority of mm. 314 ff. (the triads marked 1, 2, and 3 in example 2.37), and finally by superimposition of the dominant of F-sharp above the F-sharp pedal (at number 4). For these two measures, 325-26, the ostinato motive ceases; when it resumes in m. 327, in a slightly altered form, it is under a B-major triad—the first pure triadic consonance in the section. This reverses the functions of the upper two notes of the motive, for now A is dissonant, and B is consonant. The remainder of the section is concerned with exploiting the double triadic implications of the constantly recurring motive "X."

The final subsection treats the D/B duality in a number of ways. There are four brief fanfares, marked "A," "B," "C" and "D" on example 2.37. Fanfare "A" is the first event of the subsection, and is exclusively B major; the last event is fanfare "D," exclusively D major. The two intervening fanfares arpeggiate the B-major triad, but then end on the D-major triad. Further, the four two-measure phrase members preceding the last fanfare are arranged so that they present B-major and D-major triads in alternation (numbers 5, 6, 7 and 8 in example 2.37). Thus these final measures do not just prepare for the return of *a* tonic key, but rather reestablish a D/B duality by explicitly treating the ostinato motive so that it supports on the one hand a B-major triad with A as a decorative element, and on the other, a D-major triad with B as decoration.

Once this is accomplished, the Recapitulation begins, signalled by the refrain-like recurrence of the first thematic material of the movement. This refrain must be understood as recapitulatory, whereas those earlier could not be so interpreted, because it is the only one to occur after all points of the tonal plot have been worked out by tonal articulation of B-flat, B, G, G-sharp, E-flat and F-sharp, and after extensive preparation of both aspects of the D/B complex.

The functions of the Recapitulation are threefold. It must reestablish the tonal (and thematic) context of the FTA; it must resolve the ambiguity of that complex in favor of one element or the other; it must resolve the inherent contradictions of the STA theme.

The first goal is the simplest to achieve: as we have seen, the Retransition makes the tonal preparation for a restatement of the FTA which is slightly varied—chiefly by additional counterpoint and condensation.

The resolution of the tonic complex to an unalloyed D is accomplished in three stages. In elaboration of the idea of the tertial complex in the Exposition, B-flat was developed as an extensively prolonged key area operating in structural dissonance to D, and was prepared as such in the Transition section. It will be recalled that once B-flat was reached in the Transition, no functional connection was made between that key and D; at mm. 63-64, D returned directly to B-flat. Similarly, the emergence of B-flat at the beginning of the STA directly opposed D minor and B-flat. In the Recapitulation, the section corresponding to the Transition is mm. 356-71. There are two intrusions of B-flat upon the underlying tonality of D major. At mm. 359-62, certain of the lines introduce strong scalar elements of B-

38   *Andante Comodo*

Example 2.38.   Sketch of mm. 365–71

flat, but they are always treated as dissonant non-harmonic elements within the local context. In m. 365, the dominant of D resolves "deceptively" to B-flat, as at mm. 53–54. But this time, although there is a brief tonicization of B-flat, it is perfectly clear that it is functioning within the context of D major, as part of a neighbor motion itself prolonging the dominant of D. Instead of functioning in opposition to D, the B-flat is here decidedly subordinate, has no tonic function, and is instead part of the means of establishing D as tonic at m. 372 ff. (see example 2.38).

The second stage of the resolution of the complex is of course the recurrence of the STA thematic material harmonized in D. But unlike the first occurrence at m. 29, where the harmonization was also in D, here the theme is treated in such a way that all the crucial melodic tones are harmonized consonances at the surface level.

Example 2.39 shows the theme of the STA as it appears in the Recapitulation, and invites comparison with earlier forms of this material (see example 2.27). In its melodic essentials, this final statement of the theme most closely resembles the form used in the STA of the Exposition (see example 2.27), where it was harmonized in B-flat. The differences are rhythmic adjustments, and arpeggiations which effect octave displacements. But the three crucial notes—A, C-sharp, and F—are the cornerstones of the melodic contour and are consonant at the surface. For the first time, the vital melodic features of the theme do not conflict with the harmonization: the B-flat tendencies are avoided in favor of D minor. Since the

Example 2.39.   Recapitulation of the Second Theme

Copyright 1912 by Universal Edition A.G. Copyright renewed. © Copyright 1969 Universal Edition A.G., Universal Edition, London. All rights reserved. Used by permission of European American Music Distributors Corporation, agent for Universal Edition.

inherent tonal problem of the melody is solved at once, there is no need for extensive thematic recapitulation. However, the relatively greater musical weight of the FTA recapitulation in comparison with this truncated reference to the STA material must somehow be balanced, and for that reason, the Coda is preceded by an episode with figuration distantly related to that of the STA.

The thematic derivation of this passage is certainly obscure, but less so than its tonal language. In the broadest terms, of course, D is prolonged from mm. 376–91, again from 391–97, and once more from 398–406, at which point the Coda begins. A remarkable feature of the first of these subsections is that it includes a strongly defined emphasis on A, but in such a way as to deny an implication of dominant function for the chord. Instead, the triad, embellished by ornate counterpoint, is directed towards G minor: first through the A-*minor* triad, so that the third of the triad pushes down to B-flat rather than up to D, and then through the A-*diminished* triad—when E-natural is altered to E-flat at m. 386—which functions as an incomplete dominant to G (see example 2.40). Thus the A triad is part of the contrapuntal-harmonic elaboration of an underlying motion from I to IV to I.

Example 2.40. Reduction and Sketch of mm. 376–91

The second subsection of the episode also prolongs D by elaboration of the plagal progression. Note that again C-natural (this time in the bass) initiates motion down to B-flat, but the resolution to D is decorated by passing motions. A beautiful detail is the treatment of the climactic B in m. 396 as a harmonized neighbor, emerging by voice exchange from the bass of m. 394 (see example 2.41). This has the double effect of avoiding a superimposition of B on the D-major triad, and of confirming the prolongational role of the G triad. Resolution of the 4th of the neighbor 6/4

Example 2.41. Sketch of mm. 391–98

chord before resolution of the 6th produces, however, a temporary consonant but non-functional reference to B minor. The conflict produced by a direct overlay of B and D is carefully avoided by this cadence.

The final phrase of the episode effects a reconciliation of the major and minor modes of D. Above a D-A pedal, the horns alternate between F-sharp and F-natural, with upper and lower neighbors. In m. 400, first B-flat, and then B-natural are introduced and resolved as neighbors to A. The D-minor triad is sustained under fragmentary references to the theme of the STA (which was first introduced in the D-minor section of the FTA) represented by the three crucial notes A, C-sharp and F. The A is of course consonant in this context; the other two resolve as neighbors when D minor becomes D major by chromatic alteration of the third. The D minor of the FTA is clearly put into perspective as simply a chromatic inflection of D major.

By the time the Coda (mm. 406-54) commences, then, all but one of the tonal problems of the movement have been resolved. The function of the Coda, therefore, is largely dramatic—to allow a dissolution of the rhythmic, melodic and textural energies of the movement. But there also remains the third stage of the resolution of the complex to an unalloyed D major. After an initial prolongation of the tonic triad by inner-voice motion, the E-flat clarinet enters with a last statement of motive "Y" at its original pitch-level, which therefore refers again to the D/B complex. The first attempt to resolve the returned duality is by consonant harmonization, as at m. 396, of the B. Here, however, the resulting G chord initiates a tertial succession through E-flat to B—that is, through the set of triads representing the lower thirds of the movement's principal keys, B-flat, F-sharp and D. A partial reversal of the motion is resolved directly to D major (see example 2.42).

From this point, all the melodic material is derived from a truncated version of motive "X." This figure was treated prominently in the upper

Example 2.42. Reduction of mm. 414-34

Copyright 1912 by Universal Edition A.G. Copyright renewed. © Copyright 1969 Universal Edition A.G., Universal Edition, London. All rights reserved. Used by permission of European American Music Distributors Corporation, agent for Universal Edition.

voice at the beginning of the Recapitulation in a registral preparation for these final measures. The truncation of the motive removes the B, leaving only elements of the D-major triad, decorated by passing and lower neighbor tones. The problematical upper neighbor B is missing entirely from the principal line. The B in bassoon I and harp is indeed a neighbor, but decorates C-sharp in a local dominant, and cannot therefore be construed as implying a combination of B and D triads; the same is true of B neighbor in the horns (mm. 440-43). The double-tonic implications which first emerged through the agency of the B neighbor in motive "X" have been completely avoided, and the resolution is complete.

Historically, in sonata and related forms, the structural dominant is reached by the end of the development (and often earlier), is interrupted, and then reached again near the close of the recapitulation of the STA material. There can be no question here of the Development supporting a structural dominant; the only dominants (of D) occur in the refrains, and, as we have seen, operate only at the local level. While an A triad is treated at length just before the Coda, it does not have a dominant function at any level.

One might adopt the point of view that the harmony of mm. 437-43 constitutes a structural dominant of the movement; that is a terminological convenience at best. To take this point of view is to suggest that these measures are in some sense the goal of the preceding harmonic and linear motion, that they are a vital part of the overall harmonic plot of the piece. But the tonal goal of the movement, towards which all the preceding motion has been tending is reached *before* this point, at m. 434, where the resolution to pure D major is made and affirmed. Even though it is more extended, the dominant of mm. 437-43 does not effect a stronger resolution either of harmony or of melodic descent: the scale degree $\hat{2}$ which it supports does not resolve down to tonic, but returns as a neighbor to $\hat{3}$. Indeed, the neighbor—*not* passing—function of the E has been consistently affirmed from m. 434, and is made again explicit by the oboe in the closing six measures.

The tonal scheme of the movement has evolved exclusively from the set of tertial relationships arising from the tonic complex of D and B which is foreshadowed by $\hat{5}$-$\hat{6}$ neighbor motion in the Introduction, and then developed throughout the Exposition. That complex generates not only numerous surface features, but also tonal relationships at the middle ground. Further, our interpretation shows that the articulation of the structure effects at the background level a symmetrical subdivision of the octave by arpeggiation of D/B-flat/F-sharp/D. This background arpeggiation can be interpreted as neither weaker nor stronger than the Schenkerian *Bassbrechung*: it is simply different, and the difference is one not only of shape, but also of meaning. The Fundamental Structure of classical tonality, because it generates the music itself through the voice-leading laws of tonal syntax, is an abstraction shared by all common-practice pieces. The background key-relationships which we have termed the "tonal plot" of the first movement of Mahler's Ninth may well be unique to this piece; they arise, however, from the idea of the "double-tonic complex," which, allowing as it does for the overlay and succession of tertially related tonics, is the abstraction common to most post-Wagnerian pieces.

3

Ländler

Paul Bekker has characterized the usual Mahler dance movement as "a type derived from the Schubert and Bruckner trios: almost a minuet, almost a slow *Ländler*, almost an agitated waltz."[1] How appropriate it seems to the prejudiced eye of hindsight that the last such movement Mahler completed should explicitly invoke all three types.[2] But although it is clear that the movement very neatly comprises peasant, bourgeois, and aristocratic dance types, very little else is subject to such a satisfactorily tidy solution. The movement is so complex in its juxtaposition of simplicities, so original in its uses of cliché, and so dependent upon drastically diverse — even ironic and paradoxical — elements for the establishment of its sense of unity, that it is little wonder Mahler himself had difficulties in following through the logic of the conception.

The study of compositional method is particularly difficult in the case of Mahler because of the lack of extensive sketch and draft versions for a significant body of his music. Virtually the sole exception is the Tenth Symphony, of which two excellent facsimile publications have been made. According to Andraschke, the known preliminary materials for the Ninth are a sketchbook (in private hands and not available to the public),[3] some "preliminary studies" for the second movement, some very brief sketches for the first and last movements, and the Draft Score for the first three movements. In addition, there exist Mahler's final Full Score and the *Stichvorlage*.[4]

Study of these materials reveals that, whether or not it was Mahler's usual practice (which seems unlikely), in the case of the second movement he made significant changes to the structure of the piece after finishing the Draft Score. It is apparent from the state of the existing sketches that early work proceeded on all four movements at the same time. In view of the remarkable tonal and thematic connections among the movements such a discovery is not at all surprising, but it does pose an additional problem about the changed second movement. It is certain that most of the changes were made after the completion of the Draft Score, and perhaps even during preparation of the final Full Score of the movement.[5] But it would surely be immensely revealing to know at what stage in the drafting of the later movements Mahler came to realize that the draft version of the second movement was unsatisfactory. Although the documentary evidence now known will not support even a provisional answer to this question, determination of the structural and tonal logic of the final version of the movement is greatly facilitated by reference to the Draft Score, and it is even possible to make concrete suggestions about what in the earlier version made the changes necessary.

Example 3.1. Design of the Second Movement

	90		218	261	333	369		404		523	
A	R$_{efrain}$		B	R$'_{efrain}$	B$'$	A$'$		R$''_{efrain}$		A$''$	
	(Trio)			(Trio)				(Trio)			
		148							486		
LÄNDLER	WALTZ I	WALTZ II	MENUET	WALTZ I	MENUET	LÄNDLER		WALTZ II	WALTZ I	LÄNDLER	
C	E	E$^\flat$	F	D	F	C		E$^\flat$	B$^\flat$	C	

Example 3.1 gives an overview of the design of the final version of the second movement, and illustrates the necessarily complex nomenclature developed in the course of the analysis. There is an almost universal agreement in published commentaries either to consider that the form of the movement is essentially that of a dance with two trios (perhaps modelled upon the Schumann Second Symphony, or the Brahms Second), or to ignore the problem entirely and simply to describe the succession of tempo and character changes. For example, Michael Kennedy says the *Ländler* has "two trios, in different tempi";[6] Erwin Stein considers that "tempos II and III take the place of the first and second trio, although the succession is not the usual one";[7] Hans Redlich agrees with Stein.[8] Jack Diether's view is similar, except he apparently understands the third dance as a trio to the first, with the waltz as an extraneous element. But his description of a "double Scherzo, in which a *Ländler* (Tempo I) is set in opposition to a waltz (Tempo II),"[9] clearly suggests that the waltz, too, functions like a trio of the first dance.

Andraschke has studied both the Draft Score and the final version, and states directly that "in the D.S., the succession of the three theme groups does not reveal a consistent principle of organization."[10] The one consistency Andraschke finds in the final version is that each of the three large units into which he divides the movement contains an expository statement of each of the dance types.[11] However, even in this he is mistaken, as the last representative of the third dance, the brief section from mm. 516–22, is merely a transitional reference, the importance of which he has exaggerated in order to lend support to his "slightly spurious formal scheme."[12] Example 3.2 shows Andraschke's view of the form.[13]

Example 3.2. Andraschke's Analysis

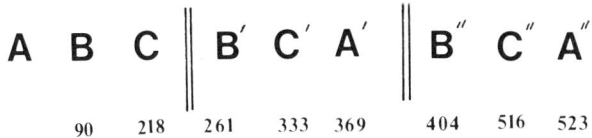

Andraschke is defensive about the problems inherent in this view, since it is the only point of the analysis for which he attempts a substantial justification: "This part has, in spite of its shortness, the weight of an independent section, for the brevity is balanced by the motivic concentration in these bars."[14] His argument is weakened by four crucial factors:

1. The passage is tonally unstable, its function being solely modulatory.
2. There is no differentiation of tempo to mark its beginning (unlike every other major section).
3. This is by no means the only instance of such motivic concentration (see, for example, mm. 168 ff.).
4. No amount of motivic concentration could compensate for the difference in musical weight between these seven measures and the more than one hundred measures of both the preceding and following sections.

In short, the main thematic succession must be seen as A-B-C-B-C-A-B-A, an arrangement which does indeed show no apparent "consistent principle of organization."

But this movement, no less than the first, is tonal music, and must therefore derive the logic of its organization from a specific tonal plan supported by the thematic structure. The crucial aspect of the tonal plan in this instance is that two of the dances are treated tonally and thematically as refrains; that is, each is associated with a single principal key: the *Ländler*

46 Ländler

with C major, and the minuet with F major. That being so, the last six in the succession of dances clearly form two thematically and tonally closed ternary units. The symmetry of this design is enhanced by the tertial key-relation established in the middle section of each large unit.

Further evidence that Mahler conceived the movement in terms of these closed units is provided by the Draft Score. Example 3.3 shows the thematic succession and tonal background of both Draft and Final versions. The essential difference in the Draft is that there the first and second, rather than the second and third, sections are closed units. It seems evident, then, that the model for the movement is a compound ternary design in which the major subdivisions prolong C, F and C respectively, and each of these prolongations exploits an upper- or lower-third relation (see example 3.4).

Example 3.3. Designs of Draft and Final Versions

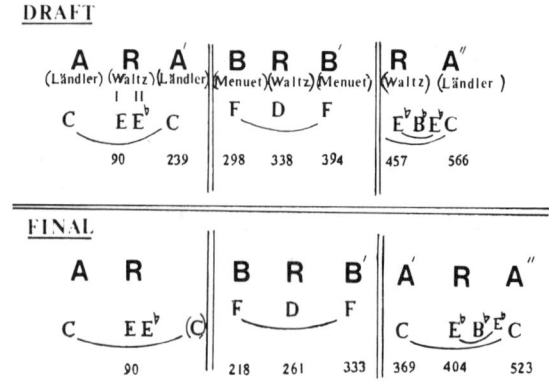

Example 3.4. Key-Plan of the Second Movement

This somewhat naive design is made more sophisticated by Mahler's truncation of one of the sections by the use of similar material (the waltz) for all three "trios," and by the tonal complexity of those trios. To understand the broader paradoxical role of the waltz—it helps provide a sense of thematic unity by appearing as trio to both the *Ländler* and the minuet, and yet must also provide on that second appearance the contrast essential to the overall ternary design—one has only to realize that Mahler has in fact provided *two* waltzes. Although the second is developed from a gesture of the first (see mm. 123 ff.), the waltzes are contrasted in motive, texture, key and treatment; Waltz I occurs each time in a different key, and Waltz II, like *Ländler* and the minuet, is not transposed. The crucial distinction for the perception of the form, however, is that the outer trios (the trios of the *Ländler* are made parallel by the use of both waltzes; the trio to the minuet omits Waltz II entirely.

Many points of detail support this conception of the structure. The transition from the first waltz section to the F-major minuet is especially revealing. The waltz material is firmly in E-flat from m. 146 to m. 187. From this point, a digression is made towards E major (this is discussed at greater length below); however, the resolution to E is avoided at m. 198 by a diversion to C major, articulated by the trumpet entry with a reference to the *Ländler* (mm. 40–45). C is then prolonged by means of the chief motive of the waltz (see example 3.10 below), and becomes a dominant of F (see example 3.5). With the resolution to F there enters, for the first time since the end of the C-major opening section, a version of the principal motive diatonically harmonized. Thus, both the path of the modulation from E-flat to F, and the explicit thematic/tonal reference recall the opening of the movement, and ensure that the entry of the F-major minuet is heard in that context.

Example 3.5. Reduction of mm. 187–205

Copyright 1912 by Universal Edition A.G. Copyright renewed. © Copyright 1969 Universal Edition A.G., Universal Edition, London. All rights reserved. Used by permission of European American Music Distributors Corporation, agent for Universal Edition.

If this is a valid interpretation of the broad tonal scheme of the movement, then it is reasonable to expect that the plagal prolongation it represents will be foreshadowed by earlier, smaller-scale relationships. From the opening pages of the movement and a simple schematic diagram of the design one might well infer that the recurrences of the first section are simple repetitions of utterly conventional material. Such an inference would, of course, be mistaken, since the two later occurrences of the *Ländler*, although thematically similar and fundamentally in C major, have secondary tonal implications different from those of the original section

48   Ländler

and of each other. This is so because each recurrence is heard in the context of the surrounding sections, and therefore each has a specific role to play in the establishment or resolution of various aspects of the tonal plot. It is the tonal function of the first *Ländler* to establish the principal tonal center of the movement and to foreshadow the basic plagal prolongation effected by the large ternary design.

Example 3.6.   Phrase Structure of Section 1

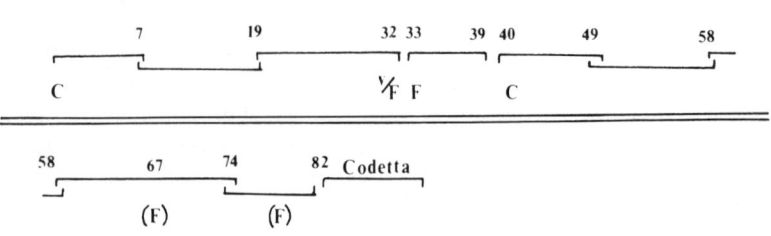

Example 3.6 illustrates the phrase structure of the opening section. It should be noted at once that however rustic the melodic and harmonic gestures may be, the highly sophisticated phrase structure belies the peasant character. Not a single phrase of the entire dance can clearly be understood to form a traditional four- or eight-bar unit, and no two successive phrases are even of the same length. Indeed, the cadential overlaps and the orchestrational manipulation of motives are so subtle that the constant elisions make precise isolation of individual phrases virtually impossible. Thus the section assumes, in spite of its harmonic simplicity, almost the character of continuous additive variations. Only three clearly defined cadential caesuras punctuate the dance, but all three—at mm. 32, 39, and 80—are vital.

The third cadence, at m. 80, functions as the true close of the *Ländler* section; the phrase which follows provides only a coda-like motivic dissolution, with the final harmonic resolution to I interrupted by the onset of the waltz. The other two cadences serve to demarcate a single phrase in the middle of the section. This phrase itself prolongs F major, established in the

Example 3.7.   Plagal Prolongation, mm. 30-40

Copyright 1912 by Universal Edition A.G. Copyright renewed. © Copyright 1969 Universal Edition A.G., Universal Edition, London. All rights reserved. Used by permission of European American Music Distributors Corporation, agent for Universal Edition.

Ländler 49

⁶/₄ position, thus effecting a larger neighboring plagal prolongation of the surrounding C major (see example 3.7).

Although the dance closes with two more brief references to a tonicized F, the effect is different in each case. At mm. 66–69, the F functions as a pre-dominant, rather than as a neighbor to C, and at mm. 76–78 the tonicization is actually illusory, arising solely from the melodic shape in the line of the violin I (see example 3.8). Thus the section contains only one real secondary tonal point — the prolonged F major of mm. 33–39 — and exhibits the same large-scale harmonic plan as does the movement as a whole.

Example 3.8. S.S., mm. 66–70 and 75–79

Copyright 1912 by Universal Edition A.G. Copyright renewed. © Copyright 1969 Universal Edition A.G., Universal Edition, London. All rights reserved. Used by permission of European American Music Distributors Corporation, agent for Universal Edition.

Since this kind of foreshadowing is useful only in the early stages of the piece, the two later recurrences of the *Ländler* are harmonically quite different; they have nothing to do with F as a secondary tonal area, but instead take part in the tonal events initiated by the waltz episodes.

Example 3.9. Themes of the Three Dances

Copyright 1912 by Universal Edition A.G. Copyright renewed. © Copyright 1969 Universal Edition A.G., Universal Edition, London. All rights reserved. Used by permission of European American Music Distributors Corporation, agent for Universal Edition.

50   Ländler

It has been well established that, although they contrast on the surface, the three dances share a common motivic germ, which can be traced back to the principal theme of the first movement (see example 3.9). In addition, Diether and Rivier point out that the version given by the waltz, which will be designated hereafter as the Refrain or "motto theme" of the movement, directly foreshadows the theme of the Finale.[15] Diether goes farther, however, and remarks that "the long-term significance lies in the chord-progression as well as the melodic outline, and extends over three movements."[16] The presumption is that he is referring to the last three movements, since there are explicit occurrences of the idea in the third movement at mm. 109 ff., and throughout the fourth. But the *harmonic* idea (hereafter designated the "motto progression") is in fact crucial to all four movements. As example 3.10 demonstrates, the motive originates in the development section of the *Andante Comodo*.

Example 3.10.   Origin of the Motto Progression

Copyright 1912 by Universal Edition A.G. Copyright renewed. © Copyright 1969 Universal Edition A.G., Universal Edition, London. All rights reserved. Used by permission of European American Music Distributors Corporation, agent for Universal Edition.

It is surely an intentional part of Mahler's plan that the second and third appearances of the "waltz version" in the second movement are in D and B-flat respectively, and thus are, in effect, "out-of-phase" versions of each other and of the original pattern in movement I: all three versions arpeggiate through D, B-flat and F-sharp. Indeed, as we shall see below, the use of this motive in the third movement provides a precisely analogous preparation for the Adagio.

There is a second problem posed by the waltzes. As we have seen, Waltz I is a point of common motivic ground with the rest of the movement and also provides certain tonal links to other movements. But it is Waltz II which provides the clues to the tonal plot of the *Ländler*/Trio sections, and therefore to the revisions of the Draft Score. The principal tonal planes of the movement can best be understood as exploiting the relationships of upper and lower thirds. The most straightforward expression of this intent is the middle section: Minuet in F major, Waltz I trio in D major, and reprise of Minuet in F. This is not a classical major/relative-minor pair, but two major keys a minor third apart. As a further reflection of this relation the strong secondary key of A major is established in the first minuet.

Example 3.11 shows the direct juxtaposition of F major and A major, aurally the most prominent feature of the passage. The modulation back to F is accomplished in such a way that A functions almost in the classical sense as a divider between tonic and dominant (see example 3.12); nonetheless, the effect of the structural balance is that the A major supports a principal section, and B-flat is merely transitional.

Example 3.11. S.S., mm. 227-31

Copyright 1912 by Universal Edition A.G. Copyright renewed. © Copyright 1969 Universal Edition A.G., Universal Edition, London. All rights reserved. Used by permission of European American Music Distributors Corporation, agent for Universal Edition.

Example 3.12. Background, mm. 218-52

Not only the Minuet/Waltz I, but also the *Ländler*/Waltz II expresses the tertial relationship. This is clearest in the final third of the movement, in which the *Ländler* (mm. 369-404) is followed — after a short transition — by an extended treatment of Waltz II in E-flat, including a developmental middle section in G-flat (mm. 445-65). The point of the reversal of order of the two waltzes in this "recapitulatory" part of the movement is to allow a direct juxtaposition of the the C and E-flat materials, thus providing a balance for the corresponding relationship in the Minuet/Waltz I unit.

This scheme is obscured by the lengthy return of Waltz I (mm. 486-512), but comparison of the Draft Score with the final version again reveals the origin of Mahler's design. The entire Waltz II/Waltz I complex (mm. 423-512) is taken without essential change from the draft version (mm. DS 457-547). In the draft, the transition to the final C-major *Ländler* occupies twenty measures (mm. DS 546-66), of which the most notable feature is a return of the Waltz I in E-flat (mm. DS 551 ff.). Thus the Waltz complex as a whole is ultimately simply in E-flat; the B-flat section does not represent a progression away from that tonality, but rather operates as a conventional dominant to prolong it.

Example 3.13 gives a reduction of the corresponding transition in the final version. Although considerably shortened, and without direct motivic reference to Waltz II, the section prepares for the entry of the final *Ländler* through a passage which is essentially a dominant prolongation in C, but which refers to the minor as well as the major mode in order to allow implication of E-flat. The new transition therefore not only retains—in far more subtle terms—the crucial reference to E-flat, but does so in a context which foreshadows certain aspects of the succeeding section as well.

Example 3.13. S.S., mm. 512-22

Copyright 1912 by Universal Edition A.G. Copyright renewed. © Copyright 1969 Universal Edition A.G., Universal Edition, London. All rights reserved. Used by permission of European American Music Distributors Corporation, agent for Universal Edition.

Clearly the function of Waltz II in its first appearance is also to express C and E-flat, even though the balancing C-major return has been truncated (see p. 46, above). The strong E-major statement of Waltz I is more difficult to understand. Of course, just as in the first movement both B and B-flat received expression as lower thirds to D, here the occurrence of E may superficially be accounted for as a representation of the "other" upper third to C. Certain reservations must be made, however. In particular, it seems important that, unlike E-flat, this key does not return, find new expression, and then resolve to the principal tonic. Furthermore, with this one exception, the tonal plot of the movement appears to be concerned with *minor-third* oppositions: C/E-flat; E-flat/G-flat; F/D. Such a prominent use of E as well as E-flat would seem to call for a corresponding use of both lower thirds to F in the middle section; but D-flat is conspicuously absent in this movement.

The E-major Waltz I seems "wrong" in two other respects: the details of its melodic structure and of its harmonization. Example 3.14 illustrates

Example 3.14. Versions of Waltz I

(iii) mm. 113–19 essentially equivalent to (i) except that m. 117 (cf. 94) has 7th chord on F.

(iv) mm. 119–23 a rhythmically compressed version of (ii).

Copyright 1912 by Universal Edition A.G. Copyright renewed. © Copyright 1969 Universal Edition A.G., Universal Edition, London. All rights reserved. Used by permission of European American Music Distributors Corporation, agent for Universal Edition.

the various treatments of its chief motive. Although in both other Waltz I sections the melodic descent is *always* from the third scale degree, here that melodic form alternates with one which descends from the tonic.

The first "octave-descent" version is harmonized in a complex, chromatic, but essentially common-practice manner. The first chord of m. 91 establishes a pre-dominant harmony; the bass line then descends from an inner-voice F-sharp (m. 92), in a line broken by voice-exchange with the uppermost part, to the dominant (see example 3.15). The second strophe[17] of the dance (mm. 113 ff.) uses a virtually identical harmonization for this melody; the only difference here is that the descending tendency of the

Example 3.15. Sketch of mm. 90–96

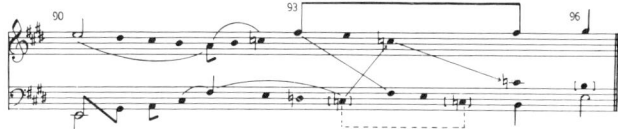

lower voice is intensified by a lowering of the F-sharp to F-natural when it is transferred from the upper voice (at m. 117, corresponding to m. 94).

In both first and second strophes, the consequent phrase, a harmonization of the step-descent from $\hat{3}$, exemplifies Bekker's remark that while Mahler's harmony seems at times amazingly naive (as, for example, at the opening of this movement), at others "it seems unfathomable in its ornate complexity of various tonal elements."[18] Note, for example, that while the melodic descent is now "correctly" from $\hat{3}$, and the harmonization begins like the model progression (arpeggiation through major thirds, each decorated by a lower-semitone appoggiatura), the F-major chord of m. 98 interrupts both the melodic descent and the harmonic progression. That progression concludes two beats later as a slight variation of mm. 93–96. It is thus clear that the passage is prolonging E major, doing so in part by a bass descent to the dominant, and in part by embellished arpeggiation. The problem is that the connection between the two processes, the progression of mm. 96–98, seems inexplicable in any conventional terms of harmonic or contrapuntal prolongation.

These paradoxes are a key to the dramatic idea of this movement of musical ironies. The ironic juxtaposition of the commonplace and the profound is one of the most remarkable and disconcerting aspects of Mahler's symphonic style. The psychological trauma apparently at its root is well documented, as is Mahler's awareness of the effect, and perhaps of its cause.[19] In any case, the "vivid contrast between high tragedy and low farce, sublimated, disguised and transfigured as it often was, emerged as a leading artistic principle in his music, a principle almost always *ironic in intent and execution.*"[20]

Mahler's life-long inclination to retrospective and introspective self-quotation is still evident in the Ninth,[21] and the "ironic intent" is manifested not only by parody of theme, but also by parody of, and conflict between, different harmonic languages. For the first time since the great compositional change marked by the Fifth Symphony, Mahler resurrects the primitive dance type familiar from the First, Second and Third; the startling stylistic contrast of the waltz serves as a large-scale paradigm for the self-parodistic manipulation of harmonic style, as the "motto" harmonization — that is, the typically Mahlerian treatment foreshadowed in Movement I and fundamental to the whole piece — gradually emerges.

This sense of "wrongness" of the way things are, and of tentative groping for what is right, leads to discontinuity and grotesquerie carried to its furthest stage in the fifth and sixth versions of the waltz theme (mm. 132 and 135 ff.). Here, metric displacement of the melodic descent gives the suggestion first of a D-major line harmonized in E, and then of the reverse: a descent in E (cf. mm. 96 ff.) harmonized in D. In neither case is the implication fully realized; the resolution of these paradoxes comes only later, when the "right" melodic descent is given the "right" harmonization in the "right" key.

Example 3.16 shows the next stage in the evolution of the waltz, the D-major trio to the minuet. Again there are two strophes, each with an antecedent and a consequent phrase. Always, the structural melodic descent is from $\hat{3}$, each time except the first decorated by displacement, giving a sense of return to the E-major (note the G-*sharp* appoggiatura resolving *down*) melodic descent over a D harmonic foundation (cf. mm. 135 ff.). The melodic disruption is severe enough to divert the harmonic progression from its D/B-flat/F-sharp arpeggiation, so that from mm. 278–81 the chordal background oscillates between triads on A-flat and C, the two other points in the model progression arpeggiating down from *E*. Then, at the last appearance of the motive, the melodic-harmonic correspondence is reasserted (though not fully restored), as the chromatic appoggiaturas are conventionally resolved against the underlying harmonic implications.

The last waltz, mm. 486–513, is in B-flat, a key area which performs two tonal functions in the movement. On the one hand, as we have seen above, the B-flat is heard as a dominant, subsidiary to the E-flat preceding

Example 3.16. Waltz in D Major

Copyright 1912 by Universal Edition A.G. Copyright renewed. © Copyright 1969 Universal Edition A.G., Universal Edition, London. All rights reserved. Used by permission of European American Music Distributors Corporation, agent for Universal Edition.

56   *Ländler*

and following; on the other hand, it relates to the previous Waltz I (in D) to reflect two of the crucial points of the local progression upon which it is founded. That this correspondence is not coincidental is shown by the final measures of the transition preparing for B-flat (see example 3.17). The powerful chromatic line of passing motions over the sustained G would make a parallel stepwise ascent in the bass through A seem to be the most natural means of achieving B-flat. The interpolated seventh-chord on G-flat allows a resolution to B-flat, of course, but in 6/4 position to provide a resolution of the chromatic descent G/G-flat in the bass. As the passage stands, the violation of voice-leading principles in the bass provides a direct aural connection of G-flat and B-flat, thus anticipating the first step in the arpeggiation which follows.

Example 3.17.   Transition to the Last Waltz I

Copyright 1912 by Universal Edition A.G. Copyright renewed. © Copyright 1969 Universal Edition A.G., Universal Edition, London. All rights reserved. Used by permission of European American Music Distributors Corporation, agent for Universal Edition.

Example 3.18.   S.S. and Sketch, mm. 486–89

Copyright 1912 by Universal Edition A.G. Copyright renewed. © Copyright 1969 Universal Edition A.G., Universal Edition, London. All rights reserved. Used by permission of European American Music Distributors Corporation, agent for Universal Edition.

Far more significant, however, is the consistency with which the basic waltz theme is treated. As before, there are four statements of the theme, but now every one is tonally "correct." Even the recurrence of the sharp-$\hat{4}$ appoggiaturas (mm. 494 ff.) fails to disrupt the simple reiteration of the fundamental harmonic pattern: always the initial gesture of the phrase is a prolongation of B-flat by symmetrical subdivision of the octave (see example 3.18).

To this point, then, the movement has exhibited a complex interweaving of tonal threads: the basic plagal neighbor prolongation and its foreshadowing, the gradual emergence through evolution in Waltz I of a direct reference to the augmented-triad arpeggiation of Movement I, and a "middle-ground" connection of the minor-third juxtapositions of C/E-flat and F/D. It is presumably the tonal-structural function of the final section of the movement to provide some sense of resolution for certain of these elements. In the present case, consideration of the function of closure exercised in the final section of the piece also leads to an understanding of the problems of the draft version.

Example 3.19 diagrams in detail the relationship between the two versions of the movement.[22] The most significant difference is that the design A-Ref-A' B-Ref-B' Ref-A" becomes A-Ref B-Ref-B' A'-Ref-A"; apparently the change involves merely a shifting of the A' section from third place to sixth. This is the view Andraschke takes, but it must be dismissed. Not only is his justification for the change invalid (see p. 45, above), but examination of the two versions shows at once that the sixth section of the final version is a newly composed variant of the *Ländler*; the excised DS third section is dismembered and incorporated into the final section of the movement. Something about the nature of that material makes it unacceptable except at the end of the movement.

Clearly, the problems with the structure of the Draft Score are tonal:

1. The first third of the movement (A-R-A) treats extensively both upper thirds to C; the second A section provides, early in the movement, a strong sense of tonal closure by its return to C, and by the extensive treatment of E-flat resolving to C.
2. The function of the secondary area F is ambiguous, as the neighbor is left unresolved.
3. As a concomitant of (2), there is no balancing sense of recapitulation; the final one-eighth of the movement does not allow sufficient musical space for the dissolution of the tonal activity of the first 550 measures.

Example 3.20 gives the broad harmonic scheme of the *Ländler* return (A') in the Draft Score and shows the transition leading to it in more detail.

58 Ländler

Example 3.19. Comparison of Draft and Final Versions

	Draft Score		Remarks	Final Version		
A	Ländler	1–89	Substance Retained	1–89	Ländler	A
R	Waltz 1	90–147	Substance Retained	90–147	Waltz 1	R
	Waltz 2	148–197	Substance Retained	148–197	Waltz 2	
			Essentially New	198–217	Trans.	
	Trans.	198–217	Retained: 309–327			
	Trans.	218–238	Discarded			
A′	Ländler	239–244	Discarded			
		245–260	Retained: 539–554			
		261–280	Discarded			
		281–294	Retained: 555–568			
		295–297	Discarded			
B	Minuet	298–338	Retained as 218–260 + 241–242	218–260	Minuet	B
R′	Waltz 1	339–386	Retained as 261–303 – DS 354–5 and DS 371–3	261–303	Waltz 1	R′
		387–393	DS 387–93 Replaced by 304–8	304–308		
			New	309–328	Trans.	
				329–332	Trans.	
B′	Minuet	394–428	Substance Retained	333–367	Minuet	B′
			New	368		
	Trans.	429–436	Discarded			
			New	369–403	Ländler	A′
R″	Waltz 2	437–509	Retained: 404–485	404–485	Waltz 2	R″
	Waltz 1	510–546	Retained: 486–512	486–512	Waltz 1	
		547–565	Discarded			
			New	513–522	Trans.	
A″	Ländler	566–579	Retained	523–536	Ländler	A″
		580–618	Discarded			
			New	537–538		
				539–554		
		619–629	DS 619–29 and DS 600–05 Generate 569–577	569–577		
		630–673	Substance Retained	578–621		

The most significant feature of the *Ländler* proper is the oscillation between the two modes of C, followed by a repetition of the principal thematic material in E-flat (mm. DS 249 ff.). This and the ensuing modulation back to C *major* effectively intensify and then resolve the tonal opposition of C/E-flat presented in the first two sections of the movement.

Example 3.20. Reduction of mm. DS 194–278

Copyright 1912 by Universal Edition A.G. Copyright renewed. © Copyright 1969 Universal Edition A.G., Universal Edition, London. All rights reserved. Used by permission of European American Music Distributors Corporation, agent for Universal Edition.

A number of factors support the contention that Mahler realized that this resolution had happened too early and decided to revise the Draft. This transition section is by far the most complex in the movement, and that is because it seems unsure of its tonal direction. If the goal of the transition is indeed C, then m. DS 202 should mark the re-entry of the *Ländler*. But after a twenty-measure modulation from E-flat to C, at m. DS 224 the music plunges back into E-flat with a recollection of Waltz II, and then moves again to C at m. DS 239. Of course, this is to provide preparation for the direct C/E-flat juxtaposition of mm. DS 239–58, and the transition, too, becomes part of this premature summation. In the revised version, mm. DS 198–217 of this transition are retained by Mahler and become mm. 309–27. The transferred passage has nothing to do with E-flat; it modulates to C, which in the new position functions as V of the ensuing F. All E-flat portions of the draft transition are discarded.

Mahler's uncertainty about key even at this late stage of the compositional process brings forth a question which cannot be answered unless access is gained to even earlier stages of the compositional work. At m. DS

60   Ländler

Example 3.21.   Facsimile of Draft Score p. II/19

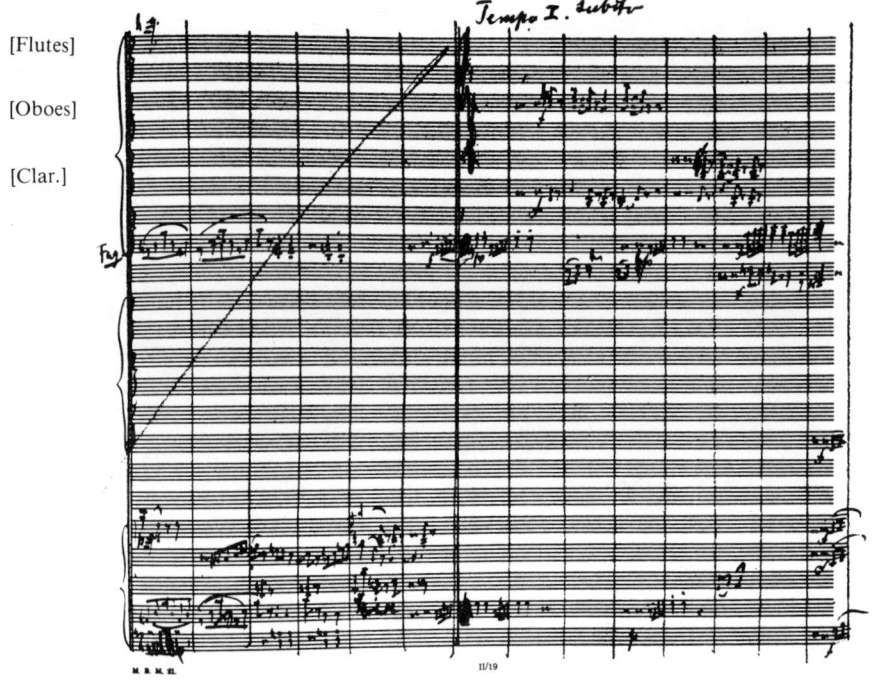

© bei Universal Edition A.G., Wien, und Internationale Gustav Mahler Gesellschaft, Wien. All rights reserved.

239, the return of the *Ländler*, Mahler apparently wrote a cancellation of the preceding key signature of three flats (see example 3.21). This change was later stricken, and accidentals altering the mode were added in oboe (m. DS 240) and clarinet (m. DS 243). They appear to have been made no later than upon completion of that page of the Draft. The changes are in heavier pen strokes than most of the notation, and the accidentals are far larger and bolder than usual; on the other hand, all pitch notations on the following pages (except for outright erasures) seem to have been entered at one time. It is impossible to say without further evidence whether the key signature was simply a slip (Mahler may for a moment have thought he was at the section beginning m. DS 258, where the change *should* occur), or whether it is an indication that even during notation Mahler was doubtful that modulation to E-flat did in fact belong here.

It is certain, however, from the nature of the changes to the final *Ländler*, that the question of the C/E-flat relationship is the principal

Ländler 61

Example 3.22. S.S., mm. DS 580-92

Copyright 1912 by Universal Edition A.G. Copyright renewed. © Copyright 1969 Universal Edition A.G., Universal Edition, London. All rights reserved. Used by permission of European American Music Distributors Corporation, agent for Universal Edition.

factor in the revisions. The last section of the Draft (mm. DS 566 ff.) corresponds roughly to the last section of the final version (m. 523 ff.); the only substantial difference is that mm. DS 580-619 are omitted and replaced by the material transferred from mm. DS 245-60 and DS 281-94.

Example 3.22 gives a reduction of mm. DS 580-92.[23] At m. DS 592 the Draft shows continuation of the cello line in G (mm. DS 595-96 in the bass are heavily stricken and replaced by a similar line—also in G—in bassoon and contrabassoon). From m. DS 598 to DS 619 the music remains entirely in C minor/major.

The twelve measures of example 3.22 begin in C and progress to G. Included are several occurrences of the principal theme; that assigned to the trombones at mm. DS 590-92 is circled (in pencil?) and may have been intended for insertion after m. DS 594. These entries of the crucial $\hat{3}$-$\hat{2}$-$\hat{1}$ descent confuse the harmonic sense of the passage. The first entry ("A" in example 3.22) is in A-flat, resolving to E; entry "B" begins in G minor, and resolves to E-flat; "C" is in E-flat. The ensuing modulation from E-flat through G to C is clumsy, and the Draft reveals that Mahler indeed had some difficulty.

The motto theme is treated similarly in the opening measures of the final version of the *Ländler*, those taken over almost intact from the Draft Score. The four occurrences of the motive are shown in example 3.23. In each case, the first *Ländler* theme, in C, occurs as a linking refrain. But unlike the discarded section quoted in example 3.22, this passage is highly concise in its tonal references. There are allusions to the two basic aspects of the broad tonal plot. The third entry (mm. 532-33) recalls the F-major neighbor of the first *Ländler* and the minuets. Although the melodic

62 Ländler

Example 3.23. Motto Theme in the Last *Ländler*

Copyright 1912 by Universal Edition A.G. Copyright renewed. © Copyright 1969 Universal Edition A.G., Universal Edition, London. All rights reserved. Used by permission of European American Music Distributors Corporation, agent for Universal Edition.

descent could have been harmonized diatonically in F (like the first in C), Mahler makes the minuet reference more explicit by the invocation of A major acting as an implied divider of the approach to the dominant (cf. mm. 227–52). Note as well the abortive references to E-flat: in the clarinets at mm. 528–29, where the resolution is to C major, and in the woodwind *tutti* at m. 535–36, where the resolution to E-flat is simply ignored and the strings continue in C major.

To produce this limited and significant set of tonal references, Mahler made one change as he transferred these measures from the Draft to the final version. In the Draft, the first statement, in the oboes, occurs in E major, resolving to C major. But this key has not nearly the same long-term significance in the movement as do F and E-flat, and thus, in the final version, the motive is in C major/minor, providing increased tonal stability at the beginning of the section, and at the same time foreshadowing the change of mode in mm. 538 ff.

Example 3.24. S.S., mm. 539–53

Copyright 1912 by Universal Edition A.G. Copyright renewed. © Copyright 1969 Universal Edition A.G., Universal Edition, London. All rights reserved. Used by permission of European American Music Distributors Corporation, agent for Universal Edition.

Mm. 539–53 are given in reduction in example 3.24. This passage and the one it replaces develop essentially the same motivic materials, all variants of the *Ländler* themes. The crucial difference is tonal. The final version does not modulate to G, nor does it superimpose the motto theme in "foreign" keys. Rather, there is a subtle overlay of E-flat and C in the classic manner of the double-tonic complex. In particular, note that while the bass in mm. 540–42 arpeggiates the E-flat triad and then descends conventionally to the dominant of that key, the violin exploits an appoggiatura with delayed resolution to state a line just as conventionally in C minor. This disparity is corrected in m. 543 with the resolution of the appoggiatura, but only to introduce another C-minor implication in the $\hat{3}$-$\hat{2}$-$\hat{1}$ horn descent. Mm. 545–47 sustain V of E-flat; the resolution at 548, however, is to E-flat colored with a suspended C in the flutes and then in the violins (see example 3.25). The C is then reaffirmed as the tonic by change of mode to C major; no further reference is made to E-flat tonic.

Example 3.25. Sketch of mm. 539–51

The final paradox of the piece is that this movement, which opens with a C-major statement in the simplest possible common-practice language, and then introduces a powerful contrasting statement in E major as the apparent secondary tonality, turns ultimately upon a duality of C and E-flat—upon precisely the sort of tertial complex exposed in the opening measures of the first movement.

The revisions of the movement after the completion of the Draft Score (shown in detail in example 3.19, above) always affect passages either in C or E-flat or which modulate from one of those keys to the other. By omitting the third dance of the Draft Score (the second *Ländler*, in C), Mahler made the progression from C to E-flat the essential tonal motion of the first part and avoided the strong sense of tonal closure which was inappropriate so early in the movement. That *Ländler* could not simply be transferred to become the first dance of the third part since there, too, it would provide too strong a resolution. Therefore, the second *Ländler* of the Final Version (mm. 369–403) is newly composed, and large portions of the omitted dance are included instead in the coda to the whole movement. Here, together with newly composed and more explicit references to the C/E-flat tonal pairing, they provide at last an appropriate and necessary resolution.

4
Rondo-Burleske

If the *Rondo-Burleske* is indeed Mahler's "most modern movement,"[1] then precisely what is the nature of that modernity, and to what degree do the technical aspects of this movement differ from those of the rest of the symphony? Although the thematic design and tonal plot are surely not classical, neither are they particularly forward-looking. Not only are they consistent with the preceding movements, but they perform a crucial role in preparing for the *Finale*. The difficulties lie in understanding and interpreting the often highly dissonant counterpoint which comprises the greater part of the movement. It is the concentration of dissonance at the surface which contributes most to the apparent modernity of the music, but it is of course essential to the artistic integrity of the whole symphony that the language should comprise an intensification of familiar techniques rather than introduce new syntactic principles.

Even in the common-practice period, the rondo is a formal principle encompassing a very large variety of specific designs. The number of parts, their disposition, and the key-scheme may all vary widely. The only invariant characteristic of the rondo is the "statement of a passage of music, the refrain, and its return at intervals after contrasting episodes";[2] normally, all occurrences of the refrain are in the tonic, and the episodes (except, perhaps, the last) in other keys.

Mahler's *Rondo-Burleske* conforms well enough to this general model (see example 4.1), but a number of anomalies must be noted. The refrains are interesting since only the first begins unequivocally in the tonic and only the last closes in that key. The refrains are concerned not simply with prolonging the key of A, but with progressing from A to D. This aspect of the tonal plot assumes even greater significance when we note that the large third episode, which occupies approximately one-third of the playing time of the movement, is principally in D, and even the other two episodes have strong implications of D in their later stages. Furthermore, while classical rondo design often allows for the last episode to be in the tonic in a sonata-like recapitulation,[3] it is certainly not usual for the *second* episode to be in the tonic (major) also.

Example 4.1. Design of the Third Movement

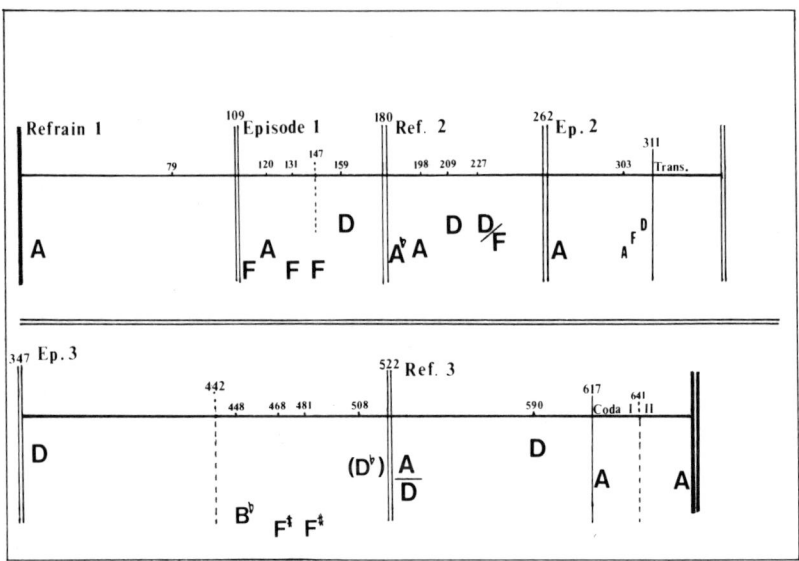

The key to these irregularities is precisely the immense third episode, set off so strikingly from the rest of the movement by texture, melodic content, rhythm, harmonic rhythm, tonal plan—in short, by virtually every stylistic characteristic. Since the very fact of this drastic sense of contrast is crucial to the episode's function and to the movement of which it is a part, it is necessary first to study the language of the refrains and the first two episodes.

We have noted that this movement is perceived as more "modern" than the others because of its accumulation of dissonance at the surface, but that accumulation occurs by means of specific techniques familiar from the other movements and does not introduce new syntactic principles. These techniques are:

1. Double-tonic complex realized by:
    a. Superimposition of two tonic triads.
    b. Superimposition of melodic strands implying different tonics.
2. Metric displacement resulting in:
    a. Superimposition of tonic and dominant functions.
    b. Superimposition of other functions.
3. Very rapid changes of local triadic center, whether that triad is actually stated or merely implied.

4. Extended passages with few simple triads.

5. Rapidly changing diatonic partitioning of the scale to correspond to local functional or non-functional triads.

6. Complex cross-relations.

7. Notes in passing or other elaborational lines given a "textural" rather than a functional or linear harmonization.

8. Passing elaborations not related diatonically to the scale of the local tonic or of the triad prolonged, but derived from a chromatic principle, such as symmetrical subdivision.

Example 4.2. Design of Refrain 1

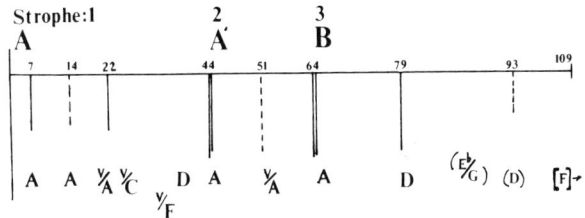

Example 4.2 shows some details of the structure and tonal design of the first refrain. It should be noted at once that the contrapuntal texture, in conjunction with numerous elided cadences, gives rise to a design with very few clearly defined subdivisions; this is particularly true at the end of the larger sections, where the transition passages are almost never independent of the main unit. Nonetheless, subsections are defined by the traditional means of rhythmic, textural and motivic articulation supporting the tonal scheme.

In the first refrain, that tonal scheme is for a strong establishment of A, which moves towards C as dominant of F, and then to D. The six measures of introduction prepare in an especially subtle way for the principal key and in doing so, foreshadow certain other important elements. The passage can be interpreted as being focussed upon D-flat, because of the strength of the opening motive, the quasi-cadential arrival at m. 4 on the dominant of D-flat, and the brass reinforcement of D-flat in m. 6 (see example 4.3).

Example 4.3. Sketch of mm. 1–7

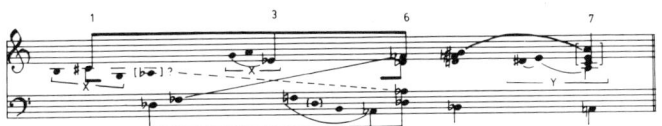

68   Rondo-Burleske

Example 4.4.   Two Interpretations of mm. 1-2

D-flat will indeed be important in this movement, but never as even a temporary tonic; D-flat is always part of a transitory progression. The whole-tone connections of the trumpet motive "x" assure that D-flat is unstable from the beginning. Mm. 1-2 thus can easily be heard as an elaboration of the half-diminished seventh chord on C-sharp, which has both implications shown in example 4.4.

The sense of D-flat as III of A and VII of D is interwoven with an implied authentic cadence in A. As example 4.5 shows, the horn pitch of m. 3 may be interpreted as leading-tone to E. Mm. 3-5 arpeggiate the E dominant ninth chord in the bass; the D-flat is a disjunct passing elaboration which divides the interval from E to B-flat. The notated B-flat seventh chord may be understood as either an appoggiatura chord to A, or as an altered form of the E ninth chord.[4]

Example 4.5.   Sketch of mm. 1-7

Both interpretations of the passage are "right" in that both sets of implications are crucial to the movement and to its role in the symphonic structure. The use of D-flat as III of A (and as VI of F) recurs throughout the movement; the A/D-flat/F series of major thirds is the foundation in several senses of the first and second episodes and provides links to the Finale as well. The introduction itself is a direct preparation for the Finale, since the tonal change from the third movement to the fourth reverses the progression of these opening measures. At the same time, it is important to hear the suggestion of the dominant of A underlying the passage, since a conventional dominant function operates at the *middle-ground* more consistently in this movement than in any other except, perhaps, the first. And lastly, since we have already noted how prominent a motion from A to D will be in the *Rondo-Burleske*, the implication of the dominant of D in the first two measures is equally important.

The first phrase of the refrain proper asserts a conventional dominant prolonging A minor by bass arpeggiation. In m. 9, the part-writing seems

Example 4.6. Sketch of mm. 7–14

awkward (the arpeggiation B/G-sharp/F recalls the bass-line of mm. 3-4), but the voice-leading is clear: G-sharp is a lower neighbor to A, and F an upper neighbor to E. The strong dissonance of m. 8 underlines an important point. The trombone statement of motive "x," because of its context, gives to the D-sharp the second, more abstruse of the two meanings ascribed to it in the introduction: it functions as a leading-tone appoggiatura to E in m. 9. The second half of the phrase is harmonically straightforward, since the simplicity of the lower voices facilitates interpretation of the decorative motions in the upper parts (see example 4.6).

The second phrase, mm. 15-22, seems at first simply to reinforce A minor with a conventional fifth-progression to A in m. 20, followed by a half cadence. But the third of the dominant triad is omitted (m. 22), since the chord also serves as a link to the following phrase in C and the complex of C and A is prepared from the beginning of the phrase. Example 4.7a shows the primary implication of the passage. After this plagal prolongation of A, symmetrical subdivision (partly elaborated by passing motion) takes the bass to A-sharp. A conventional progression leads back to A, and then, through simple passing motion, down to E, the assumed dominant. Certain details, particularly those involving rhythmically displaced decorative features, suggest other interpretations. For example, the passing chord elaborating the unfolded third within the plagal prolongation in m. 15 is placed so that it sounds like a C-major triad tonicized by the preceding incomplete dominant ninth—an impression strengthened by the parallel thirds in the bass implying a move to C/E. The C and E in the violins

Example 4.7. Sketches of mm. 17–22

(anacrusis to m. 16) serve both as anticipation of the A-minor triad in m. 16 and as a delayed resolution of the B-D from the dominant of C.

Example 4.7b shows a possible interpretation of mm. 15 and 16 in C. G-natural appears throughout the passage—even as a lower neighbor to A—save only very briefly in m. 19. Because of this, the return to A minor in m. 20 gives rather more the impression of vi in C than of i in A, an impression continued in the harmonized descent through G and F to E.

Example 4.8. Implications of C and A in mm. 22 ff.

In m. 23, the bass initiates a long intermittent pedal G, which functions ultimately as V of C, but also allows continuing reference to the tonal ambiguity of the preceding phrase. When one first hears this new phrase following the open fifth of the cadence, the impression is of a dominant in A (example 4.8a). As the passage continues, one quickly adjusts from a sense of G-sharp as leading-tone to A to one of A-flat as appoggiatura to the dominant of C. The resolution of that dominant naturally continues the oscillation between members of the A/C complex (see example 4.8b).

The ensuing nine measures are typical of the complex chromatic contrapuntal foreground which gives the movement such a strong sense of non-triadic modernity. The compound bass line comprises the pedal G and an inner voice (see example 4.9). There are two ascents from C-sharp; the second supplies the D and E only implied in mm. 28 and 29 (bracketed in the example). It is possible to describe all the lines as accumulations of diatonic and chromatic embellishments of a dominant seventh chord on G. For example, m. 26 as a whole is a neighboring 6/4 embellishment, within which D, B, and A in the middle voices are passing, and the C-sharp of the upper voice is a passing note with resolution delayed to the last eighth of m. 27; A-sharp is an appoggiatura to B, A-natural a neighbor to G, and C-sharp an appoggiatura to the D implied on the first beat of m. 28 (see

Example 4.9. Compound Bass, mm. 26-34

Copyright 1912 by Universal Edition A.G. Copyright renewed. © Copyright 1969 Universal Edition A.G., Universal Edition, London. All rights reserved. Used by permission of European American Music Distributors Corporation, agent for Universal Edition.

Example 4.10. Sketch of mm. 26-28

Example 4.11. Sketch of mm. 26-28

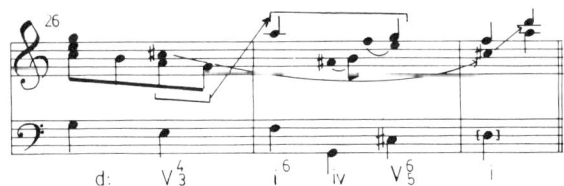

example 4.10). This view is very simple, but it adds nothing to our understanding of the music not already provided by the notion of the G pedal. On the other hand, Mahler's choice of "non-chord tones" — and especially their chromatic inflections — deliberately implies a second key area superimposed on the pedal. As always, Mahler implies secondary keys which are crucial primary keys elsewhere. From mm. 26–28, the overlaid key is D minor. The tertial unfoldings in the upper voices and C-sharp as an obvious leading-tone are unmistakable (see example 4.11). Every element of the voice-leading is correct in terms of common-practice conventions. Failure to resolve the G in the middle voice at mm. 26–27 is customary with the given bass, and in any case, the seventh is picked up in m. 27 in its *original* register, and is resolved. Even the registral transfer of the resolution of the final C-sharp has many common-practice precedents.

In m. 28, D-sharp is harmonized by the upper voices as a leading-tone to E (see example 4.12); the following measures then develop the idea of the double function of E established at the cadence in m. 22. The upper voice of mm. 30–31 arpeggiates the E ninth chord, while the inner voices with the motives marked "x" and "y" carry the implied progression by fifths to D (compare the resolution at m. 32 to that of m. 28 in example 4.11). In mm. 32, 33 and 34, the F-sharp functions in one sense as a rather odd raised-$\hat{4}$ appoggiatura in C, and in another to imply E minor in conjunction with the other voices. In spite of the long G pedal, the resolution to C in m. 34 has therefore almost the sound of a "deceptive" resolution in E (example 4.13). The G-sharp and F-sharp in m. 33 are both passing tones with their chromatic inflection derived from the scale of E, the secondary member of the complex. The technique is common enough in the earlier

Example 4.12. S.S., mm. 28-34

Copyright 1912 by Universal Edition A.G. Copyright renewed. © Copyright 1969 Universal Edition A.G., Universal Edition, London. All rights reserved. Used by permission of European American Music Distributors Corporation, agent for Universal Edition.

Example 4.13. S.S., mm. 33-34

Copyright 1912 by Universal Edition A.G. Copyright renewed. © Copyright 1969 Universal Edition A.G., Universal Edition, London. All rights reserved. Used by permission of European American Music Distributors Corporation, agent for Universal Edition.

Example 4.14. E/C Double Tonic

Example 4.15. S.S., mm. 34-38

Copyright 1912 by Universal Edition A.G. Copyright renewed. © Copyright 1969 Universal Edition A.G., Universal Edition, London. All rights reserved. Used by permission of European American Music Distributors Corporation, agent for Universal Edition.

movements (see, for example, movement I/80 ff.); here the level of dissonance, and therefore the ease with which the two keys are perceived, is increased because Mahler does not use the most compatible modes (C major and E minor), but rather C major and E *major* (see example 4.14). The tonics sounding together have only one common tone, E. Each of the two harmonic strands has its own logic; each of the lines is diatonically based in one key or the other. The result is a highly dissonant texture with an unstable sense of tonic.

One reason for this instability is that C is never more than a temporary goal in this movement, and it always prepares for one or both of the two most important secondary keys, F and D. Inner-voice motion from m. 34 first tonicizes F and then a parallel ⁶/₃ descent through a sixth prolongs it. The A thus achieved functions both as $\hat{5}$ of D and as $\hat{3}$ of F (see example 4.15).

The D-minor triad is prolonged by simple unfolding in the bass, over which the sixth-descent of example 4.15 is varied in the upper voices. Again the final degree of the linear descent serves as common tone and becomes the seventh of the dominant of E, in turn the dominant of A, preparing for the second strophe. This modulation illustrates a technique of harmonic concentration found at many other important structural points in the movement. Mm. 42–43 are vertically a simple dominant seventh chord on B, but the trumpet reiteration of motive "x" (example 4.16) superimposes upon that chord its resolution to E and then A (cf. mm. 6–7). In m. 44, the A functions as tonic, not as the seventh of B; D and B are passing. A still simpler interpretation of the passage would regard m. 43 as superimposing V/E and E, and m. 44 as superimposing V/A and A: the dominant and its resolution occur simultaneously rather than consecutively.

Example 4.16. Sketch of mm. 38–45

The second strophe of the refrain is a free variant of the first. Mm. 44–56 correspond to mm. 7–19 with some differences of rhythm and harmonic-contrapuntal detail; the latter elaborate and clarify certain of the earlier passages. For example, m. 46 confirms that m. 9 is simply part of an unfolding downward of the tonic triad; mm. 52–53 show that our interpretation of the plagal prolongation of A in mm. 15 and 16 is correct. The continuation of the first strophe led from a B-minor triad (m. 19) to an ambiguous half cadence in A, which served as a link between E (as V of A)

74 Rondo-Burleske

Example 4.17. Source of mm. 56 ff.

Copyright 1912 by Universal Edition A.G. Copyright renewed. © Copyright 1969 Universal Edition A.G., Universal Edition, London. All rights reserved. Used by permission of European American Music Distributors Corporation, agent for Universal Edition.

and C (as, eventually, V of F); the long developmental passage then led again to a strong dominant of E. In the second strophe, the functions of the two B triads are combined. That is, m. 56 corresponds to m. 19, but now the harmony is prolonged by an augmentation of the repeated bass motive (mm. 41-43) and leads again to a recurrence of the principal idea in A (see example 4.17). The upper voices are arranged so that while prolonging the B seventh chord they allude as well to the triads of E (m. 56), F (m. 57), D (m. 58), and C (m. 59) — the four degrees tonicized in mm. 23-43.

The cadence of Strophe 2 (mm. 60-63) is a more elaborate version of mm. 42-44. It has the same overlaid tonic and dominant functions, but the dominant is more explicit as a melodic superimposition on a tonic 6/4 chord (m. 63), and it is decorated (or displaced) by embellishment derived from m. 6 in order to strengthen the return to A.

Example 4.18. Sketch of mm. 66-71

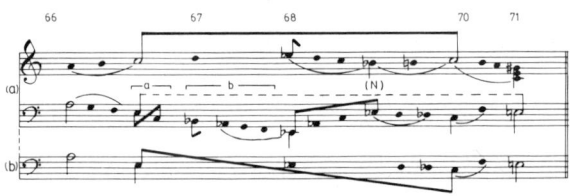

Two nested bass descents from A to E provide the framework for the first phrase of Strophe 3 (mm. 64-71); the first E is interpreted as $\hat{3}$ of C, the second as $\hat{3}$ of C *and* $\hat{5}$ of A. The background of the passage predicates this duality (see example 4.18b). The first E is prolonged as the upper member of an unfolded third which supports the dominant of F, itself a

Rondo-Burleske 75

neighbor to E. The unfolded third is foreshadowed in m. 66 (see motive "a" in example 4.18a), and then prolonged by chromatic passing motion. The first passing note, E-flat, is itself the subject of two prolongations—by tonicization (m. 67), and by plagal extension (m. 68–69). All of m. 67 of course functions as dominant of E-flat. The apparent tonicization of G is an incidental result of inner-voice motion harmonizing the passing tones in the bass (motive "b"). The final event in the phrase explicitly invokes both functions of E, as the cadential chord combines elements from both triads.

Phrase 2 (mm. 71–75) extends the complex by prolonging the E-major triad, but always resolves it to F, and interjects as well a strong tonicization of the dominant of C. Thus, like the closing measures of the first strophe, the passage overlays implications of the dominants of A and F, and the establishment of F prepares the modulation to D (see example 4.19). In the second strophe, this is accomplished through a variant of the cadential formula of mm. 6–7 and 64–65, with the A thus achieved acting as V of D; the horn line in mm. 76–77 is derived from an anticipation of the diatonic scale of D.

Example 4.19. Sketch of mm. 71–79

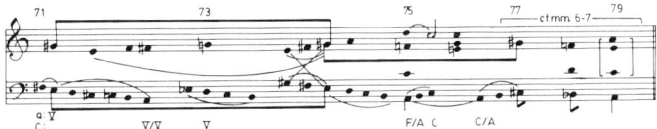

With the strongly articulated entries in D, the second half of the strophe begins in m. 79. After four measures of straightforward D minor, the intensely disjunct counterpoint plunges into a complex of E-flat and G, the tonal sense established as much by the diatonic implications of fragmentary lines as by triads. Example 4.20 presents mm. 85–88, with harmonic reductions interpreting first the strong G minor of the upper line and then the equally strong E-flat of the bass.

The equivocal function of the bass entry (marked "y" in example 4.20a) is particularly interesting. The line is an exact transposition up a perfect fourth of the D-minor woodwind entry of m. 79, and thus presumably implies G minor (see example 4.20b). The trumpet entry (marked "x") reinforces G; but the E-flat in the top voices effectively reverses the functions of the C-sharp and D in the bass (example 4.20c). All voices *except the trumpet* resolve to IV of E-flat, which continues normally to m. 90. The trumpet line of mm. 88–89, as a transposition of the principal motive of the movement, is in G minor (see example 4.21). Even in m. 90, E-flat appears in the top voice as a $\hat{6}$–$\hat{5}$ displacement over the bass G, just as it had done in m. 88.

The trumpet line not only threads a strand of G minor through the

Example 4.20. S.S., mm. 84-88

Copyright 1912 by Universal Edition A.G. Copyright renewed. © Copyright 1969 Universal Edition A.G., Universal Edition, London. All rights reserved. Used by permission of European American Music Distributors Corporation, agent for Universal Edition.

Example 4.21. Mm. 6 ff. and mm. 88 ff.

Copyright 1912 by Universal Edition A.G. Copyright renewed. © Copyright 1969 Universal Edition A.G., Universal Edition, London. All rights reserved. Used by permission of European American Music Distributors Corporation, agent for Universal Edition.

Example 4.22. Sketch of mm. 88-101

predominantly E-flat texture, but also establishes the functional bass note G, which, as the most important common member of the G/E-flat complex, is the subject of prolongation from m. 88 to m. 95. The bass line is unremarkable, and simply unfolds the G/B-flat third common to the two tonic triads (see example 4.22). A beautifully subtle reinterpretation of A-flat ($\hat{4}$ of E-flat in m. 96) as G-sharp (leading-tone to A in m. 98) underscores the point that in both measures the bass A-flat is passing from G to A, but in the first instance the chord it supports contradicts its linear meaning. The three-note-motive entries of mm. 94–98 are specific indicators of the harmonic duality. The violins (m. 94) present the V of E-flat, but the final note is harmonized by G minor, under which the bass arpeggiates E-flat; the trumpet motive is immediately answered by horns in E-flat, but the violins already anticipate what follows and outline G minor as the subdominant of D (see example 4.23). The whole passage, from m. 79 to m. 100, prolongs D by means of an extended fourth scale degree, which in turn is prolonged as an intricate complex of G and E-flat.

Example 4.23. S.S., mm. 94–96

Copyright 1912 by Universal Edition A.G. Copyright renewed. © Copyright 1969 Universal Edition A.G., Universal Edition, London. All rights reserved. Used by permission of European American Music Distributors Corporation, agent for Universal Edition.

A brief transition, mm. 101–07, prepares for the first episode. The immediate approach is made from D-flat, functioning as VI of F, as we saw above. The sense of D-flat as III of A is significant in the introduction, and we shall see in the discussion of the episodes that the reversal of the relation here (D-flat as *lower* major third of F) completes an important aspect of the tonal plan. Superimposed on D-flat is a concentrated reference to the tonal world left behind. The fifth and seventh of the D-flat chord serve also as the third and fifth of the E-major triad, which—as in mm. 71–78—works as V of A and alternates with V of C; and through all this, the trumpet foreshadows the theme of the ensuing episode, but in D minor (see example 4.24).

The second refrain exhibits several peculiarities of design, tonal plan and melodic and harmonic details. Like the first, this refrain comprises three strophes, begins in A and moves to D through the intermediary third,

Example 4.24. S.S., mm. 104–8

Copyright 1912 by Universal Edition A.G. Copyright renewed. © Copyright 1969 Universal Edition A.G., Universal Edition, London. All rights reserved. Used by permission of European American Music Distributors Corporation, agent for Universal Edition.

Example 4.25. Design of Refrain 2

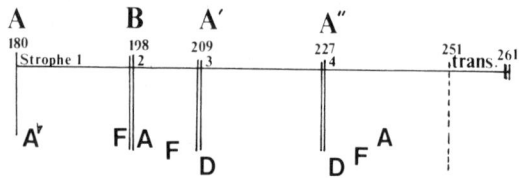

F. However, this structure is preceded by a long introduction in A-flat which has all the thematic characteristics of a self-contained strophe within the refrain. This opening strophe is a contrapuntal *tour de force*, not so much newly composed as it is assembled from transposed lines taken from both earlier occurrences of the thematic material (the beginnings of Strophes 1 and 2 of the first refrain); the result is quadruple (invertible) counterpoint. Example 4.26 shows the source of each of the lines or textural streams. Other than transposition, practically no variation of material is made. There are two exceptions, one trivial and the other significant. The descending scale in quarter-notes, transferred from m. 9, is embellished with off-beat eighths, but the sense of the passage is not altered. The bass line in m. 191, if an exact transposition of the source (violins, m. 55), would read as shown in example 4.27b. The E-natural (example 4.27c), tonicizing F, prepares for m. 196, where the F seventh chord replaces the B-flat required by strict adherence to the model.

The B-flat prolonged through mm. 56–59 prepares the return to A, as at mm. 6–7. Clearly, m. 198 is a variant of this formula, but the harmonic interjection of m. 197 makes it appear that the resolution will be to F (F-sharp is here an upper neighbor to F). The first chord of m. 198 may function with any of its notes as root, and may therefore represent F, resolving m. 197; A, anticipating m. 199; and D-flat, the usual member of this recurrent progression (see example 4.28).

Strophe 2 (mm. 199–209) derives from strophe 3 of the first refrain.

Example 4.26. Sources of Refrain 2

REFRAIN 2		REFRAIN 1			
		Strophe 1		Strophe 2	
Bass/trmb	180–191			Hns	44–47
then Vlc, w.w.				Vln	47–55
Bass	192–195			Bass	56–59
Trumpet	180–81	Vln	7–8		
Horns	182–83	Ob/trpt	9–10		
Horns	184–85	New			
Horns	186	(Bs/Vlc	13)		
Vln chords	188–91			Trmb	52–55
Vla/Vlc	180–83	Bs/Vlc	7–8		
Trumpet	185–87	Horns	12–14		
Fl/Vln	180–81			(New)	
Fl/Vln	181–87			Bs/Vcl	46–41
Woodwind	188–91			New	

Example 4.27. M. 55 Compared with m. 191

Copyright 1912 by Universal Edition A.G. Copyright renewed. © Copyright 1969 Universal Edition A.G., Universal Edition, London. All rights reserved. Used by permission of European American Music Distributors Corporation, agent for Universal Edition.

Example 4.28. Sketch of mm. 192–99

Comparison of the two reveals a fascinating middle-ground identity. In both cases, E, prolonged by an unfolded third decorated by chromatic passing tones follows the stepwise descent of a fourth. In example 4.29a the first of those tones is itself the subject of an extended prolongation. Both times, the C-major chord functions as V of F, but example 4.29b shows that the resolution is prolonged exactly as the earlier passage had prolonged E-flat (compare "w" with "y" and "x" with "z" in example 4.29). Each time, the F resolves as an upper neighbor and continues to D.

Example 4.29. Sketches of mm. 66–71 and mm. 199–204

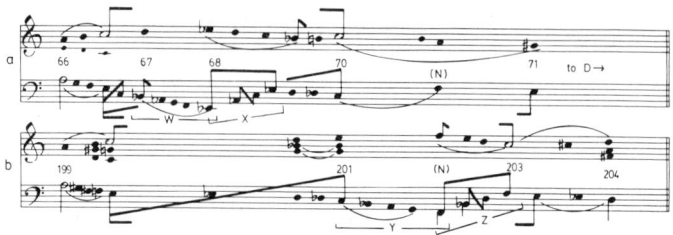

After m. 203, unlike the earlier treatment, the progression to D is immediate. The simple plagal decoration of m. 204 is diverted by an irregular resolution of B in the upper voice, which allows two important allusions. First is an anticipation of certain aspects of the third *episode*, with its association of B-flat, F-sharp and D (note especially the bass arpeggiation in mm. 205–6); then the B-flat resolves up as a leading-tone to give a tonicization of B, the last important tonal element in that same episode. The chords in m. 208 derive from consonant harmonization of the passing motions in the outer voices, but the F-sharp chord leading from the B-flat implied in m. 205 to the D of m. 209 again expresses the set of three conjunct major thirds (see example 4.30).

Example 4.30. Sketch of mm. 204–9

Strophes 3 and 4 (mm. 204–26 and mm. 227–50) are founded on a complex of D and F; D is the primary member. The language here seems quite conventional except for the freedom with which tones are embellished. In particular, we note the use of the leading-tone as an incomplete neighbor to the sixth degree, itself a neighbor to the dominant. Even more interesting is the function of A in the passage. A sketch of the bass line alone (see example 4.31) would make it appear that the passage exploits the common-practice arpeggiation from a minor tonic through the relative major as a divider to the dominant. However, in the realization of the bass, A never functions as dominant of D, but always as part of a secondary complex with F. The leading-tone C-sharp in m. 213 *resolves* as the minor sixth of F. The

Example 4.31. Sketch of mm. 209–27

Example 4.32. S.S., mm. 224–27

Copyright 1912 by Universal Edition A.G. Copyright renewed. © Copyright 1969 Universal Edition A.G., Universal Edition, London. All rights reserved. Used by permission of European American Music Distributors Corporation, agent for Universal Edition.

C-sharp in m. 216 is immediately contradicted as violins and flutes state the main melody in A minor, and the bass of m. 217 supports an implication of both F and D. Finally, both the sequential progression and the arrangement of the upper voices recall the F/A complex in mm. 224–26, but the presumed resolution to F is supplanted by D minor for the beginning of the next strophe (see example 4.32).

The fourth strophe, mm. 227–43, is a variation by invertible counterpoint of Strophe 3. In general, the upper and lower voices are simply exchanged; inner parts are only occasionally retained, and for the second half of the section are essentially newly composed. Example 4.33 shows the derivation of the common material.

Example 4.33. Comparison of Strophes 3 and 4

STROPHE 3			STROPHE 4
Trmb/Vlc	209–12	227–30	Ob/Cl/Trmp
Cl	210–12	228–30	Hn/Bsn
Vla/Vlc/Trmb	213–15	231–33	Ob/Cl/Vla
Clar/Vln II	213–15	231–33	Hn/Bsn/Vlc
Fl/Vln I	216–25	234–43	Vlc/Bs
BCl/Bsn	217–23	235–41	Vln I/Fl
Vln II/Vla	216–17	234–35	Vln II/Vla
Vln II/Vla	219–20	237–38	Vln II/Vla
Vlc/Bs	218–23	236–41	Fl/Vln I
Vlc/Bs	224–25	242–43	Vln I

Example 4.34. S.S. and Sketch, mm. 244–45

Copyright 1912 by Universal Edition A.G. Copyright renewed. © Copyright 1969 Universal Edition A.G., Universal Edition, London. All rights reserved. Used by permission of European American Music Distributors Corporation, agent for Universal Edition.

At mm. 239–40, the chromatic inflection of the bass line is altered in order to strengthen the F side of the complex. In keeping with the resultant weakening of A, the inner voices (woodwind and middle strings) of m. 242 are new, and change the meaning of the bass line completely so that the entire measure now functions as dominant of G. This change is crucial since sequential treatment makes m. 243 (derived from m. 225) the dominant of F—resolving to D. The D thus achieved is prolonged by arpeggiation through major thirds, reflecting the augmented chord above the first G. These final measures before the transition leading *from* the D-minor half of the refrain therefore parallel exactly the passage which led *to* it (see examples 4.30 and 4.34).

The last refrain derives its language and most of its content directly from the first two, already discussed in some detail above. The chief interest to the analyst is a consideration of its role in the tonal structure, and this is best treated only after the intervening episodes are understood. The first two episodes are heard as "trios" to the tonally more complex and texturally more intense refrains, and that "trio" character is reflected in the close similarity between the content of these sections and the waltz-trios of the second movement.

A simple diagram of the thematic design (example 4.35) shows that Episode 1 comprises two strophes of three periods each. The corresponding periods of each strophe contain similar melodic material, but although both begin in F, the harmonic plans are different. The notion of tonal contrast essential to the idea of the rondo episode is realized in an original way: the principal tonal areas of the first episode are also those of the refrain, but are

Example 4.35. Design of Episode 1

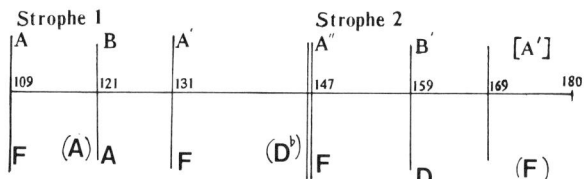

rearranged so that F becomes the principal key, and first A and then D the secondary third-related areas (cf. examples 4.35, 4.2 and 4.25).

The overall tonal plan of the first strophe—a movement from F to A with a reassertion of F—is foreshadowed by the structure of the first period. A conventional background motion from I-V is elaborated by III (A major) as a divider, but a parallel motivic structure and the progression through descending major thirds (familiar from the second movement) give special prominence to the arrival of A. The interpretation of A as an important goal is given added weight by the use of that same progression to prepare for the extended A major of the second period (see example 4.36). A particularly beautiful detail is the way in which the change of mode in F (major to minor) at m. 117 in preparation for D-flat is reflected by the change of mode in D-flat (major to minor) at m. 119 in preparation for A.

The prolongation of A through the second strophe is unremarkable except for one detail. In the first three measures, the leading-tone G-sharp is treated as a neighbor to $\hat{6}$, itself a neighbor to $\hat{5}$. In m. 130 this same G-

Example 4.36. Sketch of mm. 109-20

Example 4.37. Major Third Progressions

sharp is picked up, but now sounds also as the minor third of the ensuing F, and thus directly reverses the motion which originally led *from* F. The function of the period in A as the extended last stage in the symmetrical division of the octave F/D-flat/A/F is therefore underscored (see example 4.37).

The first eight measures of the last period (A′) are a simple variant of mm. 109–16; the next four measures then briefly prolong the lower third, D-flat, instead of the upper third, A. This balancing tonicization of D-flat not only realizes, at a slightly deeper level, the foreground progression through major thirds, but also foreshadows the relationship between the two strophes of the episode. The harmonic plan thus exposed is essentially that of the Minuet/Waltz/Minuet section of Movement II.

The first period of Strophe 2 corresponds melodically and tonally to mm. 109–18. There are, however, great differences in the harmonic-contrapuntal details. Measures 147–48 prolong F, but do so through the medium of inner-voice motion over a sustained bass F; the "motto progression" through major thirds enters only at the end of the period. In spite of this great difference of surface technique, the passage retains the change of mode crucial to its source; the cadence is upon F, however, rather than A, to make the tertial relationship clear (see example 4.38).

Example 4.38. Sketch of mm. 147–59

Example 4.39. S.S., mm. 166–69

Copyright 1912 by Universal Edition A.G. Copyright renewed. © Copyright 1969 Universal Edition A.G., Universal Edition, London. All rights reserved. Used by permission of European American Music Distributors Corporation, agent for Universal Edition.

Tonal contrast in the first strophe is provided by the upper third of the tonic; the second strophe inverts that relationship by transposing its second period down a perfect fifth from the original level. The tonic pedal is retained, and although the inner voices are very different, the passage presents a simple contrapuntal prolongation of D. As in the corresponding passage of the first strophe, modulation to the initial chord of the next period is made through reinterpretation of the function of the leading-tone treated first as a neighbor (horns, m. 160), and the C-sharp then recurs to anticipate the chord of m. 169 (see example 4.39). In the cadential progression of Period 2, sonority "a" is passing and "b" a functional chord; viewed retrospectively from Period 3, that interpretation is reversed.

Example 4.40. S.S. and Sketches, mm. 177–79

Copyright 1912 by Universal Edition A.G. Copyright renewed. © Copyright 1969 Universal Edition A.G., Universal Edition, London. All rights reserved. Used by permission of European American Music Distributors Corporation, agent for Universal Edition.

Because of the harmonic and melodic elisions, the final phrase of the episode appears to be in D-flat. In fact, mm. 169–76 are almost identical with mm. 131–39; the only significant difference is that the opening progression through descending major thirds to A begins at the second step. The plan of the whole second strophe, with its successive periods in F, D and F, is encapsulated in mm. 177–79 (see example 4.40). Consideration of only the abstract relationship of the outer voices gives the interpretation shown in example 4.40c, but the details of the realization place registral, motivic and metric emphasis on the first beat of m. 178 and justify the sketch given in example 4.40b.

Episode 2 is a freely derived variant of Episode 1: the themes, figurations and occasional fragments of the whole texture are similar, but there is no wholesale transfer of material as there had been between the first two refrains. We have already noted both superficial and substantial parallels between the episodes of this movement and the trios (waltzes) of Movement II. An important part of the design of that movement is that the last two waltzes, in D and B-flat, reflect in their relationship the sequence of major thirds, a prominent harmonic progression there as in the *Rondo* episodes. It is therefore not surprising that the first two of those episodes are tonally related in similar fashion.

Example 4.41. Design of Episode 2

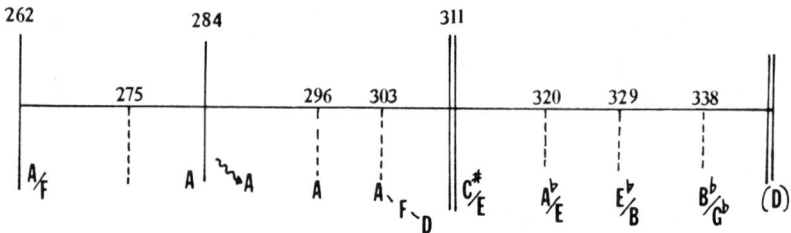

Example 4.42. Sketch of mm. 262-75

Example 4.43. S.S., mm. 264-67

Copyright 1912 by Universal Edition A.G. Copyright renewed. © Copyright 1969 Universal Edition A.G., Universal Edition, London. All rights reserved. Used by permission of European American Music Distributors Corporation, agent for Universal Edition.

Example 4.44. S.S. and Sketch, mm. 289-96

Copyright 1912 by Universal Edition A.G. Copyright renewed. © Copyright 1969 Universal Edition A.G., Universal Edition, London. All rights reserved. Used by permission of European American Music Distributors Corporation, agent for Universal Edition.

The first period of the second episode is closely derived from mm. 147-59: the underlying harmonic plan is a simple prolongation of A effected by contrapuntal passing motions (example 4.42). Although there is no explicit invocation of the motto progression, F—the first intermediate goal of that progression—is strongly implied as a secondary point of focus. The caesura at the end of the first phrase segment marks the arrival on F, and the upper voices from mm. 264-67 are derived from F major/minor (see example 4.43). Although the melodic line is transposed up a third for the second phrase (mm. 276-83), the chief linear and harmonic implications again refer to the A/F complex.

Harmonic and melodic elision like that so common in the movement's refrains overlap the cadence in A with the beginning of the next phrase in A-flat. The A-flat triad, however, simply initiates the motto progression, now through E and C, and an abrupt return of A at m. 288. The next eight measures, while "in A," are the most complex in the episode. The sense of A is provided by the sustained pedal, triadically realized at both ends of the phrase (mm. 288 and 295). The background motion is that of a neighbor chord reflecting the cadential formula of mm. 6-7. Note the detail of the oboe/violin II entry in m. 295, underscoring the reference.

Measures 288-90 are complicated by the overlay on A of two other triads—the C major from m. 287, and the C-sharp which is tonicized by inner-voice motion; that tonicization completes the parallel to mm. 4-7. The superimposition of a C-major triad draws attention to the "dissonant" sonority of m. 288, and links it to that of m. 295. That in turn suggests that the octave displacement of G-sharp in the violins at m. 295 is to ensure that G-sharp is heard not just as a suspension, but as the fourth tone of a four-note chord—a vertical expression of the arpeggiation from m. 282 (begun with coincident implications of G-sharp and A) to m. 288 (see example 4.45).

Example 4.45. Reduction of mm. 281-96

While the final phrase of the episode (mm. 296-303) seems to reestablish a single tonic triad, the bass octaves of the cadence conceal an anticipation of the later tonicization of F. The ensuing brief transition encapsulates the harmonic plan of the first refrain—exploitation of the complexes of A/F and F/D. A is given by the harmonic cadence (mm. 302-3) and is one of the possible tonal implications of the trombone entry (mm. 308-10); the continuation of the line by the horns tonicizes A at m. 318. F is implied by

88   Rondo-Burleske

the melodic approach to the cadence, by the figuration in upper woodwind (mm. 304–10), and is also encompassed by the trombone entry. But the trombone line, especially when considered in the context of the horn continuation, also may be interpreted in D. The C-sharp at m. 311 sounds at first like the leading-tone of D. At the same time, the lower line forces an interpretation in C-sharp continuing to A at m. 318.

Analysis of the trombone and horn counterpoints as implying more than one key may appear specious: the supporting texture, after all, is each time in only one of the presumed keys. The approach to the second full entry (lower strings and woodwind, m. 320) shows that the double interpretation is correct. Example 4.46 gives these measures with the bass line notated enharmonically, so that both meanings are clear. The upper voices exploit the tones of the line common to A-flat, and provide a harmonization beginning in that key; but even here, there is tonal duality. Violin II and viola partition the octave E-flat to D-sharp into whole-steps: the derivation is not from the non-diatonic idea of the whole-tone scale, but from a concatenation of diatonic tetrachords from A-flat and E (bracketed in example 4.46, second staff).

Example 4.46. S.S., mm. 318–23

Copyright 1912 by Universal Edition A.G. Copyright renewed. © Copyright 1969 Universal Edition A.G., Universal Edition, London. All rights reserved. Used by permission of European American Music Distributors Corporation, agent for Universal Edition.

The tertial complexes thus exposed govern the progress of the whole section, since it consists of four sequential statements. These begin at m. 311 (horns), m. 320 (low woodwind and low strings), m. 329 (trumpets, oboes and English horn), and m. 338 (trumpets, oboes and clarinets). Example 4.47 illustrates the harmonic succession of the whole transition.

If the tonal pattern were to continue through the last leg of the sequence, one more entry would bring a return to D-flat, the point of departure (see "Sequential Continuation" in example 4.47). Instead, the tonicization of G-flat is suggested but not fully realized, and in a reversal of the procedure by which D minor is superseded by D-flat major at m. 311, the D-flat of m. 346 is resolved as C-sharp, the leading tone of D. The

Example 4.47. Tonal Plot of Episode 2

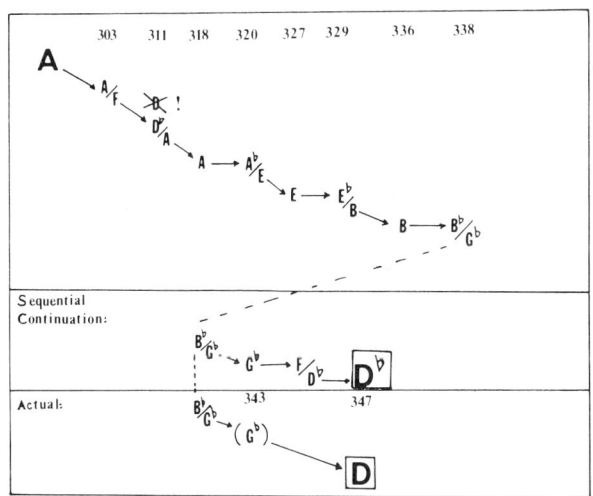

sequential transition is therefore founded at both ends upon a D/D-flat displacement; it exploits the tertial double-tonic complex, and in particular establishes a thematic contour with powerful double-tonic implications. The approach to m. 347 is through a series of major thirds, from B-flat through G-flat to D (see "Actual," example 4.47). In all of these ways, the section not only leads to, but directly foreshadows the essential features of Episode 3.

Contrasting in texture, rhythmic character, harmonic language, harmonic rhythm and intensity with the other five sections of the movement, the third episode is in all of these respects reminiscent of the first movement (see especially mm. I/317–47 and I/406–54). The motivic content consists chiefly of development of the two principal ideas of the preceding transition (see example 4.48). Motive "a" anticipates the first important motive of the Finale, but "b," a variant of the clarinet line in mm. 210 ff., is also related to

Example 4.48. Prime Motives of Episode 3

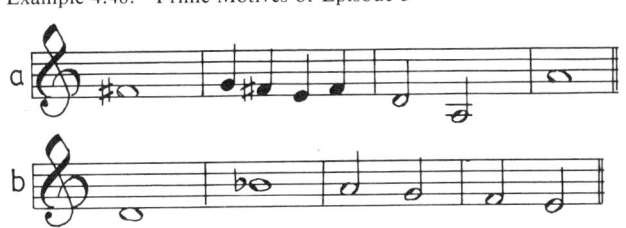

a prominent figure from mm. 8–9 of the first movement.[5] It is therefore especially significant that, like the entry in mm. 348 ff., the first four appearances of motive "b" in the movement are in D, or a complex including D (m. 210; m. 217; m. 226 and m. 227 in stretto by inversion). This specific tonal/motivic allusion and the more superficial resemblances noted above are all signals that the substance of the episode also derives directly from the first movement.

Example 4.49. Tonal Plot of Movement I

$$\begin{array}{c} D \\ B \diagup \diagdown B\flat \\ \diagdown G \diagup \diagdown F\sharp \\ \diagdown E\flat \diagdown D \end{array}$$

In that movement, the intricate sonata-form structure required exploration of the two lower thirds of each member of the background tonal succession. Consequently, only these six degrees are tonicized in the movement (see example 4.49). The third episode of the *Rondo-Burleske* parallels Movement I in the following ways:

1. Principal tonic is D.
2. The same six (and *only* those) degrees are tonicized.
3. Explicit associations link D, B-flat, F-sharp.
4. B is the last degree to be tonicized.
5. D returns throughout Part 1 of the episode as a refrain (cf. development of first movement).
6. Part 2 of the episode parallels exactly the main tonal sequence up to the end of first-movement development (without the refrains).

Example 4.50 gives an overview of the structure of the episode. Periods 1 and 2 are harmonically static, prolonging D by means of long contrapuntal elaborations. The first such motion produces, as one might expect from the recurrence of example 4.47b (in the horns), a complex of D and B-flat (see example 4.51). In purely linear terms, mm. 349 and 351 arise from neighbor motion, and the appropriate horn notes may be construed as passing. Similarly, the displacement of certain tonic and dominant elements in mm. 352–57 produces implications of a D/F-sharp complex. This subtle suggestion is explicitly realized by the violin II countermelody of mm. 362–67. Example 4.52 shows the several textural streams of the passage.

Example 4.50. Design of Episode 3

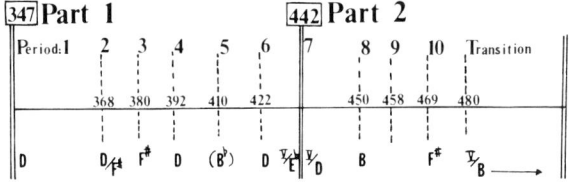

Example 4.51. S.S. and Sketch, mm. 348-52

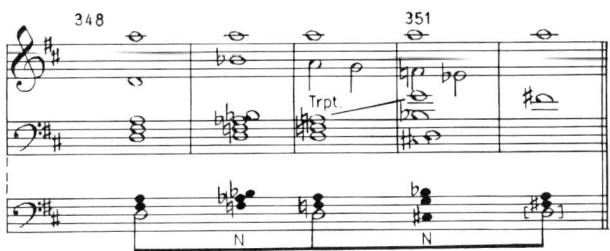

Copyright 1912 by Universal Edition A.G. Copyright renewed. © Copyright 1969 Universal Edition A.G., Universal Edition, London. All rights reserved. Used by permission of European American Music Distributors Corporation, agent for Universal Edition.

Example 4.52. S.S., mm. 362-68

Copyright 1912 by Universal Edition A.G. Copyright renewed. © Copyright 1969 Universal Edition A.G., Universal Edition, London. All rights reserved. Used by permission of European American Music Distributors Corporation, agent for Universal Edition.

The upper two staves and the lowest present no problems with their simple decorations of the D-major triad. The third staff shows the violin II part which is obviously in F-sharp, and to which the cello line (fourth staff) gives harmonic support. The sound of the two streams is absolutely clear in this eerie passage because the use of F-sharp *major* against D major allows only one common tone. The foreshadowing of later events by these incidental sonorities is completed by the secondary use of F-sharp as the dominant of B (see especially mm. 364–65 and the trumpet in mm. 374–75): in Movement I, F-sharp at the end of the development is reached as V of B and left as III of D; in Part II of this episode, it is reached as III of D and resolved as V of B.

In the ensuing periods, F-sharp and B-flat are given more extended triadic realization. In Period 3 (mm. 380–91), F-sharp is conventionally approached but resolved simply through the two tones common with the D triad (cf. mm. 352–54). The opposition of these two points of focus is affirmed by the occurrence of the same motive—a variant of example 4.48a—over both triads (see example 4.53).

Example 4.53. S.S., mm. 380–83 and 388–94

Copyright 1912 by Universal Edition A.G. Copyright renewed. © Copyright 1969 Universal Edition A.G., Universal Edition, London. All rights reserved. Used by permission of European American Music Distributors Corporation, agent for Universal Edition.

The fifth period, following a simple prolongation of D, moves to the lower thirds; here as well, the turn figure articulates the crucial tonal points. First, B-flat major—arising from a $\hat{6}$–$\hat{5}$ displacement exactly like that in Movement I/53–4—and then B (tonicized by F-sharp) are superimposed on the D-major bass. Part I of the episode then closes with the neighbor sonority which had initiated the section (mm. 348–50), but which now is approached in such a way that it sounds like a dominant of E-flat (see example 4.54). At m. 436, the A in the bassoon ceases, so the inner-voice

Example 4.54. S.S., mm. 434–38

Copyright 1912 by Universal Edition A.G. Copyright renewed. © Copyright 1969 Universal Edition A.G., Universal Edition, London. All rights reserved. Used by permission of European American Music Distributors Corporation, agent for Universal Edition.

descent from the higher octave is heard as the bass line, and the D of m. 438 does not resolve the dominant from m. 430.

The avoided harmonic resolution is, in fact, never restored. Part II begins with a D-major triad in 6/4 position, which therefore represents D as the tonic *key*, but the chord itself functions as a dominant-substitute in that key (see example 4.55). All of Part II serves as a large developmental transition back to the final refrain, with alternations of the two prime motives combined with increasingly more extensive fragments of the refrain theme. Motive "a" in D/B-flat at m. 444 is followed by "b" in B-flat (m. 450), "a" in B-flat (m. 456), "b" in G/E-flat (m. 462); contrary passing motions lead to a cadential arrival on F-sharp (m. 469), which then resolves as V of B (see example 4.56).

Example 4.55. Transition to Part 2

Example 4.56. S.S., mm. 464-71

Copyright 1912 by Universal Edition A.G. Copyright renewed. © Copyright 1969 Universal Edition A.G., Universal Edition, London. All rights reserved. Used by permission of European American Music Distributors Corporation, agent for Universal Edition.

Example 4.57. Sketch of mm. 478-80

94   Rondo-Burleske

Period 10 (mm. 469–81) prolongs B and makes its last approach to F-sharp a reminder of its broader function as part of the third-chain from D (example 4.57).

The fundamental technique of the transition is free treatment of neighbor motions, with the relationship of principal triad to neighbor several times reversed. The process is started by a development of mm. 472–75, where the neighbor motion results in the superimposition of C-major and B-major triads. The freer treatment at m. 485 sometimes obscures the strict logic of the voice leading, but comparison with the model (mm. 472–75) clarifies the meaning. The melodic lines either decorate one or more tones from one of the two triads, or make a passing elaboration of a motion from one to the other. That passing motion may be diatonic (e.g. first violin II, mm. 489–92), or chromatic (e.g. cello, mm. 489–92).

Example 4.58. S.S., mm. 472–75

Copyright 1912 by Universal Edition A.G. Copyright renewed. © Copyright 1969 Universal Edition A.G., Universal Edition, London. All rights reserved. Used by permission of European American Music Distributors Corporation, agent for Universal Edition.

In example 4.58b, the asterisk in m. 493 marks the failure of G-natural to resolve as a neighbor to F-sharp; instead, the B triad is treated as the neighbor, and resolves to C (with added seventh). The reversal of the neighbor function is echoed (with single pitches rather than full triads) through mm. 499–506. The C-major triad is now the primary sonority, but after elaboration by neighbor motion up a semi-tone, it is in turn supplanted by its neighbor (m. 508). For the last twelve measures of the transition, bass arpeggiations unfold parts of the D-flat triad (mm. 510–11), then a sonority of the D-flat/B-flat complex (m. 512–13); and finally the elements of the complex are juxtaposed in mm. 518–21, to produce a curious variant of the familiar cadence progression from m. 6 (see example 4.59).

The cadence progression thus allows for return of two keys. By its invocation—even in reverse order—of the B-flat/D-flat succession, the passage tonally prepares the return of the refrain in A for which increasingly direct motivic signals have been made. But a comparison with the transition

Example 4.59. Transition to Refrain 3

Copyright 1912 by Universal Edition A.G. Copyright renewed. © Copyright 1969 Universal Edition A.G., Universal Edition, London. All rights reserved. Used by permission of European American Music Distributors Corporation, agent for Universal Edition.

Example 4.60. Approach to and Departure from Episode 3

Copyright 1912 by Universal Edition A.G. Copyright renewed. © Copyright 1969 Universal Edition A.G., Universal Edition, London. All rights reserved. Used by permission of European American Music Distributors Corporation, agent for Universal Edition.

to the episode shows that the two passages use the same device — establishment of a D-flat triad, the root of which functions as a leading-tone to D (see example 4.60).

The duality expressed in this transition continues through the opening measures of the refrain and is representative of the principal aspect of the tonal plot — the establishment of D as the most important secondary point. The motion to D from A is usually effected through the intervening third, F. In Refrain 1, the first strophe presents this succession and foreshadows the tonal relation of the last strophe to the first two (see example 4.2); Refrain 2 uses the same plot, but with greater emphasis on D (see example 4.25). Episode 1 is constructed upon a different working-out of the F/A and F/D sets of thirds (see example 4.35). Episode 2 is almost entirely in A, but its major mode prepares the last episode, which, balanced against all that precedes it, is the largest expression of the basic idea.

Example 4.61 gives a simple graphic representation of these nested statements of the same idea. The diagram also suggests the second aspect of the tonal plot, inherent in the relationship of the episodes to the waltz-trios of Movement II. We noted in chapter 3 that the surface motion by major thirds is reflected in the starting points of the motto progression in Mvt. I/Development (G-flat), Mvt. II/2nd Trio (D) and II/3rd Trio (B-flat). In the rondo episodes, the motto progression is transposed, giving the succession F, D-flat, A (see example 4.36). Not by coincidence, the first two episodes are in F and A respectively. Thus while the D of Episode 3 satisfies one line of the tonal progression, it violates the expectations of another, which requires D-flat. We have already seen several other instances of the D/D-flat displacement, so the event is not unprepared, but the sense of incompletion is very strong. One of the functions of the Finale, as we shall see, is to resolve this aspect of the harmonic plan.

Example 4.61. Key-Plan of the *Rondo-Burleske*

R. 1	Ep. 1	R. 2	Ep. 2	Ep. 3
A ──────────────────→			A$_{major}$	D
A	F	A ──── maj ──→		D
A ──→ D	FAFDF	A→D	A	D
AFDA D				D F$^\sharp$ B$^\flat$
	F ─────────────→ A ─────→ D$^\flat$?			

Most of the final refrain consists of variation of material transferred directly from the first refrain. Example 4.62 shows the sources of these passages. There are only two large sections of new material, 5 and 11 in the chart, but some of the others contain significant changes.

We have observed how the transition at mm. 518 ff. prepares for both A and D, and how the first four measures of the episode exploit both keys. The principal theme returns, but transposed up a perfect fourth to D minor. The harmonic background of mm. 522–23 may be interpreted in both D and A, but from m. 524, A is established alone; after m. 526 correspondence to the source passage is direct. All other changes in the harmonic plan of this final refrain have the same tonal point: further reference to the A/D relationship.

Between Sections 2 and 4 are five measures (mm. 534–38) which are not

Example 4.62. Comparison of Refrains 1 and 3

Ref. 3	Ref. 1	Comment
1. 522–25	7–10 or 44–47	Significant change; see text
2. 526–33	11–18 or 48–55	
3. 534–38		New; but see text
4. 539–43	61–65	A minor altered to V/D
5. 544–60		New
6. 561–74	23–36	Last 3 mm., only one line
7. 575–79		New
8. 580–81	42–43	
9. 582–83		New
10. 584–97	79–92	
11. 598–616		New

Example 4.63. Sketch of mm. 56–62 and mm. 533–40

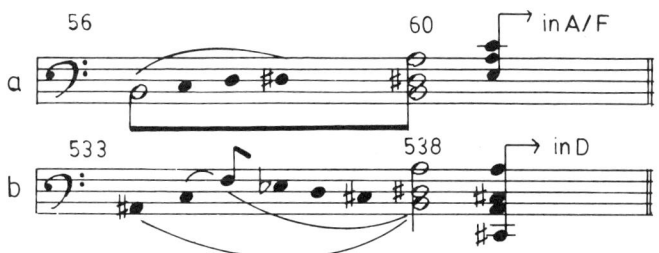

a simple variant of the corresponding source passage (mm. 56–60). None of the lines is retained, and the chordal succession is quite different, but the harmonic sense at the middle-ground is the same in both passages — prolongation of a B seventh chord. In the first instance, the prolongation is by chromatically decorated upward arpeggiation; in the second, by inner-voice descent to the chord root as the real bass (see example 4.63). At mm. 540–41 (from mm. 62–63), the trombone chord is A major rather than A minor. The point of both these changes is of course to prepare for the large new Section 5.

Motivically and texturally, there is very close correspondence between mm. 544–60 and earlier material — especially that of mm. 64 ff. — but the melodic lines are transposed (not consistently by the same interval), and the bass line is altered so that first we hear a prolongation of D and then an exploitation of E major/minor in preparation for a C/A complex in mm. 561 ff. (see example 4.64). The source for the passage in C/A, mm. 23 ff., is also approached by an E sonority with the double function of V of A and III of C. As in that earlier passage, the onset of the C/A complex in Refrain 3 turns in the bass on the interpretation of G-sharp as leading-tone of A and as lowered submediant of C.

98   Rondo-Burleske

Example 4.64.   Sketch of mm. 542–61

Example 4.65.   Sketch of mm. 613–17

Example 4.66.   Comparison of mm. 617–27 and 629–39

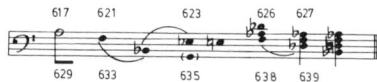

Example 4.67.   Sketch of mm. 641–55 and mm. 661–67

The last large section based on an earlier model, mm. 584–97, is in D, so the final refrain, like the first two, contains an extended section in that key; the difference here, of course, is that the tonal movement is finally closed by a transition taking the music back to A, which is then affirmed and reaffirmed in the codas. Example 4.65 illustrates that the final measures of this transition lead directly from D to A through an extended version of the obligatory cadential preparation. The two periods of Coda I are close variants of the same material—a simple progression through fourths to the D-flat triad of the cadential figure (see example 4.66).

Coda II provides the final statement of the D/A association, and at the same time places it in the context of the D/D-flat displacement noted above. Mm. 647–51 introduce a new melodic gesture tonicizing D major, and foreshadowing a variant of the cadential progression in which D supplants D-flat as the first chord (see example 4.67). The D-flat version is restored only in the last three measures and there sounds as a dissonance against the tonic note (sustained since m. 661). The D-major triad would of course seem more natural here, as it would provide a consonant harmonization. The movement thus plays out until the very end the relationships upon which so many aspects of its structure—and especially the D/D-flat displacement fundamental to Episode 3—are founded, and ends as it began, with an equivocal presentation of D-flat.

5
Finale

For the greater part of the nineteenth century, the finale remained the most difficult problem in symphonic design. Even Wagner, the master of large-scale structure, and surely the greatest musical intellect of the period, remarked late in life that if he were to turn to symphonic composition after the completion of *Parsifal*, the works must, because of the obstacle of the finale, be in one movement.[1]

Although Beethoven greatly increased the scope of symphonic design — in part because his audience was different from that of Mozart and Haydn,[2] but more because his increasingly complex tonal language required a larger space and more intense thematic development — the dramatic force remained concentrated in the first movement. Even Beethoven's conversion of the symphonic Menuet into the Scherzo, a direct reflection of the increased weight of the first movement and the concomitant need for heightened dramatic conflict in the rest of the symphony,[3] did not change the fundamental shape — an unwinding from the climactic opening movement. Beethoven in part circumvented this difficulty by attempting to balance the weight of the first movement with sheer energy, in what Bekker calls the "Apotheosis-Finale;"[4] this gives at least the illusion of an accumulation of energy from the second to the last movement.

The problem stems from the perfection of sonata form both as a musical structure ideally predicated upon the fundamental nature of common-practice tonality, and as a dramatic conception embodying conflict, evolution and ultimate resolution. It is a form both technically and conceptually complete in itself, and thus in a sense it functions not only as a part of a larger composition, but as a complete composition itself.[5]

It seems paradoxical that the three most extraordinary symphonic finales before Mahler — the Beethoven Third and Ninth, and the Brahms Fourth — are variation forms, because the variation, for lack of inherent contrast, is the "sonata's artistic antithesis."[6] But the success of each of these finales stems from the grafting onto the variation scheme of some kind of duality in which conflict is implicit. In the case of the *Eroica*, the dichotomy is thematic; in the Ninth the process is carried a step farther, and a thematic duality is overshadowed by the juxtaposition of orchestral and vocal resources; only in the Brahms IV, a Passacaglia over a theme which implies both E minor and A minor,[7] is the initial conflict primarily tonal.

However successful these devices are, none of them provides grounds for a reconception of the Symphony, or is able to serve as a general model for a new symphonic type. That new type—finally realized by Mahler—must justify the shift of dramatic high point from first to last movements by a corresponding change in the tonal process. That is, the first movement must no longer be allowed to provide a conclusive tonal closure for its own conflict, but must leave some tonal element suspended, or must initiate some tonal motion, which will attain resolution only in the finale.

Such a procedure, absolutely incompatible with common-practice tonality, is a perfectly natural exploitation of post-Wagnerian tonality. The additional dimension provided by the double-tonic complex and the multiplicity of intertwined tonal relations springing from it, allow for a (first-movement) tonal structure to be closed in one sense, but open in others.

Bruckner's tonal designs successfully encompass this new plan, but—according to Bekker—his finales are weak in conception, and thus the high point of the symphonies is shifted no later than the Adagio. Bekker says, "What benefits the first movement—every lack of consciousness of goal, of logical compulsion, whether in the whole design or in the individual themes—is a disaster for the Finale. . . . Here Bruckner failed."[8] Despite thematic cross-references and allusions, he could not attain a real concentration of structure, but remained rhapsodic. Bekker misrepresents Bruckner in several respects. His grouping of the Germanic symphonists into North German (Beethoven, Mendelssohn, Schumann, Brahms) and Austrian (Schubert, Bruckner, Mahler) schools is artificial at best: both Bruckner and Mahler owe much to Schumann and Brahms. Second, it is only in the Eighth and Ninth Symphonies that Bruckner places the Scherzo before the Adagio, and Bekker seems to underestimate the dramatic value of these powerful third movement dances. Finally, the Bruckner Finale always makes some tonal point even if it is only the reestablishment of the key of the first movement (the one possible exception, the Ninth, has no fourth movement); certainly in at least the Seventh and Eighth the Finale is not nearly so rhapsodic and unconscious of its goal as Bekker suggests.

A later example of the "Adagio-symphony" (with the same inner-movement scheme as Bruckner's Eighth is Mahler's Fourth; the last movement is, in terms of dramatic intensity, almost anti-climactic after the adagio variations, but it is absolutely necessary to complete the tonal shift from G to E prepared in both the first movement and the Adagio. It is this preparation which justifies a view of the first movement as providing only partial closure for its own tonal plot. The movement is founded upon a double-tonic complex of G and E, and provides a satisfactory resolution only for the first of the paired tonics. The Adagio, a set of double variations alternately in G and E, achieves its climax in E major (at m. 315), and the movement then closes on an equivocal dominant triad of G major. The Finale then resolves the ambiguity by beginning in G but progressing to a firm establishment of E major for the final stanza.[9]

Mahler's Second is similar in that the first movement is predicated upon a double-tonic complex (of C and E-flat), and is closed only in terms of C; it is left for the fifth movement, this time undeniably the dramatic crux of the whole work, to provide a final closure in E-flat. All the other Mahler symphonies up to the Ninth are of the same general type: they are Finale-symphonies, and the finale, "be it short, be it long, be it a broadly spun-out Allegro . . . [or] a restful Adagio . . . [is] the center to which the threads of all the preceding movements lead."[10]

A further point common to most of these works is their partitioning, either explicitly or implicitly, into two *Abteilungen*.[11] This broad division is sometimes indicated in the score, and attains its fullest realization in the Eighth, where the Adagio and Scherzo are subsumed by the Finale to form a single continuous second *Abteilung*.

The case of the Ninth is more difficult. Bekker finds that the Finale provides resolution without approaching the weight of the preceding movements, so that it is not so much a goal as an epilogic end.[12] One might counter this view with the purely subjective opinion that the emotional intensity and breadth of the last movement more than balance the weight of the others, but a more precise refutation is also possible. If the goal is *not* the Finale, then the middle movements, which surely in no way provide any sense of resolution or arrival at a goal, are inexplicable. The Ninth is unique also in that the key—and therefore the resolution—attained in the Finale is not directly prepared in the first movement, but results from relationships extending through the first three movements to the last. The Finale cannot simply be regarded as an epilogue, since it is only in that movement that the tonal goal of the symphony is reached.

The Ninth, like the Fifth, seems to have been conceived in three *Abteilungen*. The two inner movements are in many ways distorted reflections of each other—Dionysian and Apollonian visions of the same world—and they comprise a single *Abteilung*, together balancing the two slow outer movements, and providing the common ground that links those apparently disparate poles.

The principal unifying agent is, as we have seen, the harmonic "motto progression" through an octave symmetrically divided into major thirds; the cardinal points of this progression as first enunciated in Movement I are crucial tonal references in that movement and in the second; the transposed progression serves an exactly similar function in linking Movements III and IV. Example 5.1 illustrates these long-term connections.

104 Finale

Example 5.1. Tonal Connections among the Four Movements

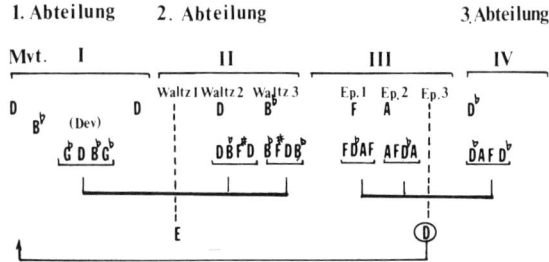

That these inter-movement relationships are part of a consistently planned scheme is shown by documentary evidence. Colin Matthews has given a description of a notebook containing sketches for all four movements of the Ninth.[13] This set of sketches shows incontrovertibly that Mahler conceived of a fully integrated symphony, not a suite of four movements; that at the earliest stages of the conception, not only the character, but also the content of each movement was already being carefully considered; and that the Adagio version of the motto theme was derived directly from the *Rondo-Burleske* version, and then simply transposed to the right key. It is evident that from the earliest stages of the creative work, the motto theme was planned as a crucial tonal and thematic guidepost.

Two elements of example 5.1 may require brief explanation. Both concern "wrong-key" statements at crucial points in the design. Very little need be added here about Episode 3 of the *Rondo-Burleske*, in which D-major and first-movement references apparently supplant the expected third motto theme in D-flat. The prime reason for this "substitution"—apart from questions of the plan of the third movement itself—is to allow the Finale to consummate the interrupted succession. In so doing, it provides resolution of the directed motion of the symphonic design in three senses: as a completion of the second motto-theme chain of thirds; as a final D-flat/D displacement in answer to the *Rondo* Episode 3; and, in far more abstract terms, as a resolution of the "structural dissonance" created by the first three movements (see example 5.2).

The other unaccounted-for item in example 5.1 is the first half of Waltz-trio I, in E—a key absolutely abandoned for the rest of the movement, where the role of upper third of C devolves upon the more usual E-

Example 5.2. Tonal Plan of the Ninth Symphony

flat. But the introductory measures of the Finale restore E to function as upper third of D-flat. The passage provides a further reference to the D/D-flat displacement since it is founded upon the same double interpretation of G-sharp (as V of D-flat and III of E) that is such an important feature of mm. 320 ff. of the *Rondo-Burleske* (see example 4.46). The E-major implication here also presents the *minor* third of D-flat, and thus prepares for the simple change of mode which gives the only prolonged tonal relief in the last movement.

These various elements of the tonal structure are left in some sense incomplete in the course of the first three movements so that the Finale has not only a dramatic, but also a musical inevitability. Indeed, because the symphony falls into three *Abteilungen*, and because the last of these large units provides both a recall of earlier thematic material and a sense of tonal resolution, it is possible to understand that the Finale assumes for the whole symphony functions similar to those of the recapitulation of a single sonata-form movement.[14]

Example 5.3. Design of the Finale

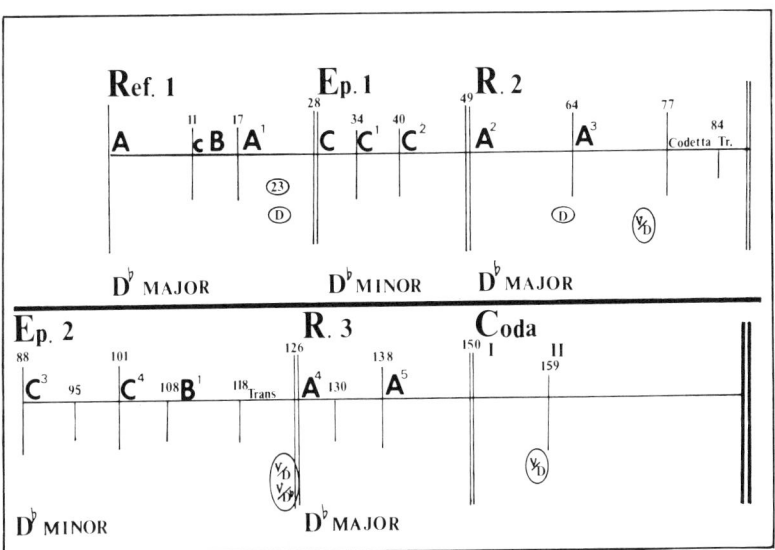

It is in keeping with its recapitulatory nature that the Finale is without extended tonal contrast; all sections of the simple five-part rondo have D-flat as principal tonic, with refrains invoking the major, and episodes the minor mode (see example 5.3), and the D-flat/D-natural displacements serve instead as the chief element of tonal tension. The contrasts of mode and theme in the episodes are carefully foreshadowed by the design of the first refrain, which at m. 11 avoids a full textural resolution to D-flat major and instead uses the opening bass line of Episode 1 as introduction to the second period. The two passages are especially interesting since they play out again the double role of A-flat in mm. 1-2. At m. 13, A-flat is the root of the A-flat triad (V of D-flat), but at m. 30, it is the third of the E major triad (III of D-flat and V of A) (see example 5.4).

Example 5.4. Two Functions of A-Flat

Copyright 1912 by Universal Edition A.G. Copyright renewed. © Copyright 1969 Universal Edition A.G., Universal Edition, London. All rights reserved. Used by permission of European American Music Distributors Corporation, agent for Universal Edition.

This first refrain is recapitulatory also in the firmness with which it asserts the principal tonic. The motto theme itself is twice altered to provide a common-practice progression that begins the first and last sections of the refrain (see example 5.5). In spite of this, two secondary features establish important links to the harmonic world of earlier movements. First is an association of B-flat with D-flat to create a double-tonic ambivalence making its appearance through a $\hat{6}$–$\hat{5}$ neighbor motion recalling the technique of the opening measures of the symphony. In m. 7, the B-flat is not simply a neighboring inflection of A-flat, but part of a B-flat triad prepared by the curious bass progression of the two preceding measures. The upper line arpeggiates the D-flat triad (but arrives on B-flat), while the lower line arpeggiates the B-flat triad (but arrives on D-flat; see example 5.6).

The bass line which began the descent to B-flat in m. 5 becomes the melodic line at mm. 13 ff.; again it introduces a D-flat/B-flat complex. In spite of the bass line in m. 13, the sense of V-I in D-flat is secondary here to the function of the B-flat triad (or, rather, B-flat/D-flat) as a neighbor, prolonged by voice-exchange, to A-flat (see example 5.7). In the two remaining occurrences of theme "A" (mm. 17 and 21), the superimposed B-flat returns, melodically tonicized by its own leading tone.

Example 5.5. Sketch of mm. 3–4 (17–18)

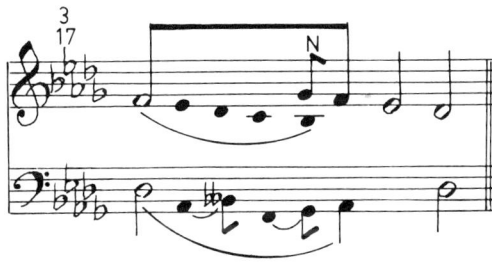

Example 5.6. Sketch of mm. 4–7

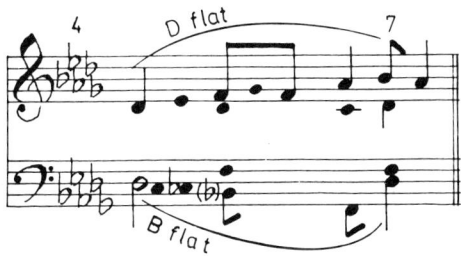

Example 5.7. Sketch of mm. 13–15

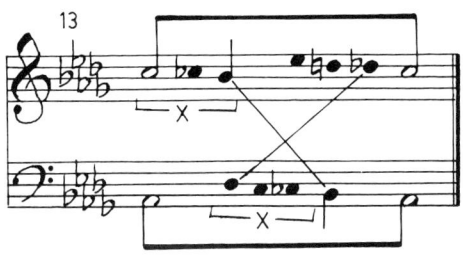

The other important secondary feature of this refrain is the peculiar treatment of the D-major triad. Here, as in each of the other refrains, climactic textural and dynamic points of tension invariably articulate arrival at either a D-major chord (simple triad or with added seventh) or a tonicization of D major. In every case the statement or implication of D resolves to D-flat, either by means of a conventional "Neapolitan" progression, or directly to a root-position tonic. The first such instance is m. 19, where, coinciding with the first *sforzando* of the movement, an abrupt violation of normal voice-leading produces a D-major triad. Note that the motive in the

Example 5.8. D Major at Climaxes

Violin II has on all previous occurrences resolved to B-flat, while the bass requires resolution to the third of the D-flat triad. Only the uppermost line is treated according to conventional expectation (see example 5.8). The progression at m. 23, coinciding with the registral peak of the whole refrain and a dramatic juxtaposition of dynamic extremes, is a more usual Neapolitan resolution, complicated only by the implied tonicization in the inner voices (example 5.8b). Finally, again as the first example of a gesture common to all the refrains, and again in the highest register, the closing measures give a taste of D overlaid on, and resolving to D-flat (mm. 24 and 26).

The slow open counterpoint of Episode 1 is ideally suited to presentation of harmonic ambiguities, and Mahler of course exploits this to allow tertial complexes stemming from the principal tonic—complexes of C-sharp and A, of A and F-sharp, and of F-sharp and D. Each of the three phrases of the episode commences in the area of the first complex and progresses to one or both elements of the last.

Already in m. 28, the long appoggiatura A in the high violins in resolution of the preceding diminished-seventh chord gives the second member of the complex sounding against the C-sharp bass line. When A is tonicized in the bass, F-sharp is immediately overlaid by the violins; then, in turn, D is suggested by the bass (m. 32) to complete the chain of overlapped thirds:

$$\frac{\underline{C^\#}}{A} - \frac{A}{\underline{F^\#}} - \frac{F^\#}{\underline{D}}$$

Phrase 2 (mm. 34–40) begins as an elaborated repetition of mm. 28–30, but a tonicization of B (m. 37) initiates motion through a descending chain of overlapped thirds to C-sharp (V of F-sharp and major I of C-sharp [minor]).

As example 5.9 shows, the last phrase of the episode begins as the first two. The C-sharp/A juxtaposition is now more sharply defined, both by the bass movement and by the repetition of the pentachord scale with D-sharp altered to D-natural (m. 41). Through mm. 42–44 the bass remains in A, but the solo violin and the third entry of the scalar motive are just as clearly in F-sharp. Mm. 44–46 complete the succession of thirds with the superim-

Example 5.9. S.S., mm. 40-49

Copyright 1912 by Universal Edition A.G. Copyright renewed. © Copyright 1969 Universal Edition A.G., Universal Edition, London. All rights reserved. Used by permission of European American Music Distributors Corporation, agent for Universal Edition.

posed D and F-sharp triads. The final transition (mm. 47-48) is based on a variant of the motto theme using combined triads for the cardinal points, and this creates the expectation of D-flat/B-flat at the beginning of the refrain (as, for example, at mm. 17 and 21). However, like the earlier numbered symphonies (and unlike *Das Lied*), this work resolves to a single tonic triad, and only in the first refrain is D-flat colored with B-flat. An analogy may be drawn to the recapitulation of the first movement, which begins by reestablishing a complex of D and B (like the exposition), but finally ends in D alone.

The second refrain comprises two principal parts based upon the motto progression, and an extended codetta. Phrase 1, mm. 49-52, is harmonically identical with mm. 17-20; the melodic variation is a perfectly straightforward alteration of the countermelodies, and the contour is unchanged. Phrase 2, a reharmonization of the motto theme, is a typical example of Mahler's chromatic passing harmonies embellishing a conventional progression (the notated F-sharp major chord in m. 54 is, of course, simply IV of D-flat). The logic is in the contrapuntal motion of the outer voices; the triads which realize this framework are incidental (see example 5.10). As if to reinforce this point, a twice-repeated cadential formula further prolongs D-flat.

Example 5.10. Sketch of mm. 53-59

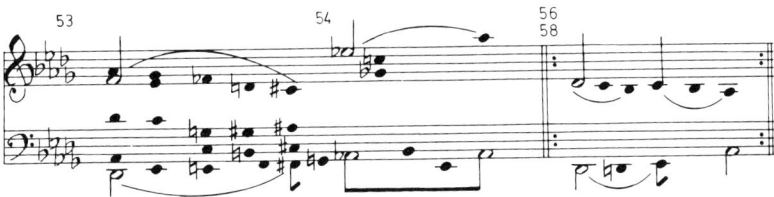

110   Finale

The final phrase of the strophe develops further the tendency noted in Refrain 1 to move at the end of a section to or towards D, with dynamic and registral intensification. Here, as always, since these moments are references to the displacement crucial to the third movement and thus also to the structural relation shown in example 5.2b, the resolution is directly to D-flat (see example 5.11). Superimposed above this is a melodic return of the E-major scale (cf. m. 2), so the resolution to D-flat encompasses two of the unresolved elements established earlier in the work.

Example 5.11.   S.S., mm. 61-64

Copyright 1912 by Universal Edition A.G. Copyright renewed. © Copyright 1969 Universal Edition A.G., Universal Edition, London. All rights reserved. Used by permission of European American Music Distributors Corporation, agent for Universal Edition.

Strophe 2 is also designed around a climactic progression to D. The most remarkable feature of the first phrase is the prolongation of IV by a double neighbor motion, enharmonically realized so the F-sharp is heard first as III of D. Indeed, the second phrase begins exactly as the first, but prolongs D (realized as a seventh chord in m. 63). The apparently random chord succession of mm. 71-73 derives its logic from the chromatic passing motion of the inner voices which elaborate the motion between the D and A triads. Of course a full tonicization of D would contradict the meaning of this movement; not only, therefore, is there a resolution from V of D to D-*flat*, but the preceding passing motion occurs in such a way that A and D-flat are linked by the fundamental progression of this symphony—a chain of major thirds (see brackets "x" and "y" in example 5.12b).

Example 5.12.   Sketches of mm. 64-68 and mm. 68-73

Example 5.13. Sketch of mm. 73-80

D-flat, thus achieved, is simply prolonged by a conventional harmonic progression (mm. 73-77), followed by a long passing motion in the inner voices. It is, of course, not at all coincidental that the register shift in that descent, articulated by the return in the viola of the turn figure (m. 79), coincides with an arrival on a D seventh chord in the upper voices ("a" in example 5.13).

Episode 2 derives its melodic materials and the chief aspects of its tonal plot from Episode 1, but after the climactic moments of the middle refrain, the treatment of D becomes increasingly more subtle throughout the second half of the movement. Two melodies, originally presented together in C-sharp and A at m. 34, are now stated in stretto, but the upper line is transposed to imply A as the V of D; the complex is unified by the harp statement of the third common to the C-sharp and A triads (see example 5.14).

Example 5.14. Openings of Episodes 1 and 2

Copyright 1912 by Universal Edition A.G. Copyright renewed. © Copyright 1969 Universal Edition A.G., Universal Edition, London. All rights reserved. Used by permission of European American Music Distributors Corporation, agent for Universal Edition.

When the bass motive reenters (now in the oboe at m. 92) in F-sharp, the upper line continues less ambiguously in D; and after a brief tonization of B-minor the lower line also introduces G-natural so that the entire texture now implies D major. The cadence and the return of the harp (now

Example 5.15. S.S., mm. 97–101

Copyright 1912 by Universal Edition A.G. Copyright renewed. © Copyright 1969 Universal Edition A.G., Universal Edition, London. All rights reserved. Used by permission of European American Music Distributors Corporation, agent for Universal Edition.

with F-sharp and A) allow interpretation in either key: the duality is expressed first by repetition of the main motive at m. 96 in D instead of in F-sharp (cf. mm. 40–41), and then throughout the last phrase of the strophe by the various lines simultaneously implying D and F-sharp (see example 5.15). Vertical alignments express the same idea when the preponderent F-sharp is supplanted by D (m. 100), and the approach to the cadence, as in the previous phrase, is in that key alone.

A triple interpretation of the harp's C-sharp/E is exploited when the second strophe begins at m. 101. As at m. 88, when the full texture enters in mm. 102 ff., the contrapuntal weaving of the lines produces a complex of C-sharp and A (but without the explicit establishment of A as V of D). Example 5.15 includes at m. 101 two bracketed notes which do not occur in the score, but are surely the understood continuations of the actual lines. Had these tendencies been realized, the resulting sonority would consist of the simultaneous triads of F-sharp and A, and this complex supports most of the second strophe. F-sharp returns first as a simple neighbor to A, through $\hat{5}$-$\hat{6}$-$\hat{5}$ motion in the harp, which is also reflected in the upper melodic line. Both triads are represented in m. 106, before a change of mode removes the possibility of interpretation in A (see example 5.16). The

Example 5.16. Sketch of mm. 102–7

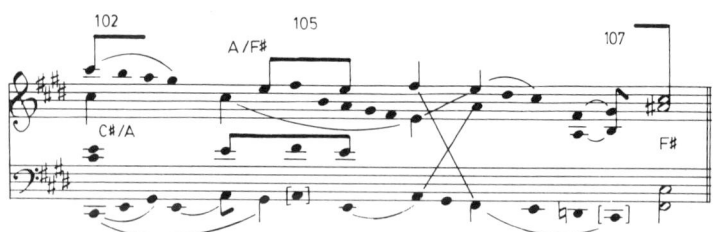

D which functions in the phrase *beginning* in m. 107 as VI of F-sharp, seems briefly to be a tonicized cadential goal of the *preceding* phrase; this is a deliberate ambiguity.

Throughout this movement, F-sharp has been used as a link between the tonic D-flat and the "sharp-side" complexes in which it is paired with A or D. This enharmonic relationship is exploited here by the F-sharp major triad which is first prolonged by its own dominant but with a strongly articulated reference to the ubiquitous D major as a passing elaboration. It then initiates a conventional progression to E-flat seventh (V7 of V in D-flat) at m. 115.

Example 5.17. Sketch of mm. 107–18; Reduction of mm. 115–17

Copyright 1912 by Universal Edition A.G. Copyright renewed. © Copyright 1969 Universal Edition A.G., Universal Edition, London. All rights reserved. Used by permission of European American Music Distributors Corporation, agent for Universal Edition.

A sketch of these measures (see example 5.17a) shows a passing chord in m. 116. However, this simplification of the texture misinterprets the significance of the sonority. Entry of the three trombones (see example 5.17b) after a complete measure's rest gives the A-major triad a considerable weight, and in the next measure the root of the dominant ninth is avoided until the last beat. Thus the existing sonority may be interpreted as both V of D (without the root) and V of A-flat (without the root); *both* roots are provided on the last quarter of m. 117.

We have noted how Strophe 2 of the second refrain is directly preceded by reference to both D major and E major (see example 5.11). The culminating measures of the transition to the final refrain, beginning at m. 118 with a five-measure dominant pedal, bring back those two crucial elements and set them both in opposition to the dominant of D-flat major. The orchestrational emphasis upon the D major is unmistakable — four horns and three trombones *fortissimo*. Against that complement, massed strings and woodwinds in octaves, also *fortissimo*, give the first pitch of the E scale, later completed by upper strings alone. There are three conflicting harmonic strands, each of which for its own reasons must give way to D-flat.

Almost as if in recognition of the power of this sense of triple resolution, the heavily scored refrain begins *fortissimo* in stark contrast to all the earlier sections. Furthermore, the harmonic elements of the transition recur, first as part of a chromatic prolongation of D-flat, and then in a now familiar pattern, as an interrupted move to D major resolving instead to D-flat. Mm. 126 ff. are a varied extension of the motto progression from mm. 64 ff. In effect, the change involves a prolongation of the D-major triad before the progression continues to F-sharp (IV of D-flat; see example 5.18). The tonal stability of D is greatly decreased by the harmonization of the upper member of the double neighbor.

Example 5.18. Sketch of mm. 126-30

The consequent phrase, a variant of mm. 53 ff., likewise temporarily implies D. A comparison of example 5.10 with example 5.19 shows that the bass passing motion in the latter avoids the subdominant function that in the first instance triggers the cadence. Instead, motion is to the V of D, which is then prolonged under a melodic line firmly in D-flat. Surface characteristics — metric emphasis and register shift — draw attention to the F-major triad, so the whole passage again places A in its most important context — as VI of D-flat and a member of the crucial sequence of major thirds, rather than as V of D.

The last phrase of the refrain proper presents the final appearance of

Example 5.19. Sketch of mm. 130–34

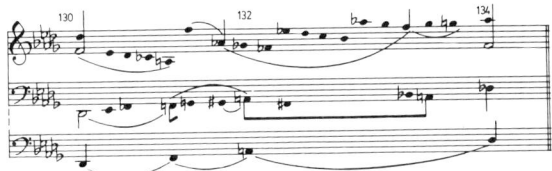

the motto progression (except for fragmented references in the coda); it is the most persistent in its attempts to avoid D-flat; and it includes the only transposition of the motto in the entire movement, if we discount the rather skeletal reference at mm. 47–48. The significant point here is that Mahler does not pursue his attempted tonicization of A as V of D (initiated at m. 139; cf. mm. 132–33). Instead of the expected A-major triad on the first beat of m. 141, the F-major triad from m. 131 is picked up again, and from here the motto progression continues and reestablishes A in the context of a chain of major thirds (see example 5.20). Passing motion then leads directly to the V-I cadence in D-flat.

Example 5.20. Sketch of mm. 138–48

Beginning in m. 148, the coda is given tonal impetus by a series of harmonic implications overlaid as conflicting elements above one authentic and one plagal extension of the cadential resolution to D-flat in mm. 145–48.

The first continuation suspends the leading tone C, which then descends through semi-tones to A-natural at mm. 153–54. The whole gesture, including the incidental sonorities of m. 148 (D- and E-major triads

Example 5.21. Sketch of mm. 148–60

under a B natural), is derived from the climactic conflation of harmonic implications in mm. 63–64 (example 5.11). The reference is intensified by two additional elements. A-natural, once achieved, supports a reiterated V of D, and the phrase continues with a diatonic descent to A-flat, but this beautiful line is diatonic in E, not in A-flat. Thus the *chromatic* descent to A as $\hat{5}$ of D is transformed into the diatonic approach that from the very first measures of the movement has always signalled D-flat (see example 5.21). This represents the final stage of the various relationships between A and D-flat which have been played out over the course of this movement: A has functioned as V of D and has had a crucial role in the D/D-flat displacement idea; it has been linked to D-flat as the penultimate member of a series of rising major thirds; and now it recedes into the surface to become a relatively conventional pre-dominant (the "German 6th") in D-flat. A last lingering pause on the sonority arises from passing and neighboring motions (see example 5.22). Note that the bass A-flat does not appear in m. 161, so that, however briefly, the A seventh chord may sound alone; and the half-bar rest allows a moment of suspense before the proper resolution occurs.

Example 5.22. S.S., mm. 160–73

Copyright 1912 by Universal Edition A.G. Copyright renewed. © Copyright 1969 Universal Edition A.G., Universal Edition, London. All rights reserved. Used by permission of European American Music Distributors Corporation, agent for Universal Edition.

The tonal plot must strengthen the role of the Finale in the whole symphonic structure. This has been done most directly by playing out at foreground and middleground levels the tonal designs shown above in examples 5.2a and 5.2b. Example 5.2c supposes a far more abstract sense of long-term dissonance and resolution, which, however, has been exploited as a surface event at crucial structural points of the Finale. It seems wonderfully appropriate that it recurs as part of the final harmonic event of the piece, and arranged in such a way that it harmonizes a suspended C, which then descends to resolution through a D-flat diatonic scale. The parallel to mm. 148 ff. is obvious (see example 5.21). This last section of the symphony allows the voice-leading to pass through only three triadic sonorities in dissonance against the underlying D-flat, and the roots of these chords represent the tonics of each of the first three movements.

The final resolution to D-flat therefore signifies the end not only of the last movement, but of the whole symphonic structure, which has unfolded as a single artistic entity through a multiplicity of tonal dimensions across the almost superficial division into movements.

Deryck Cooke has observed that Mahler "handled tonality, as did Wagner, with absolute technical mastery. . . . His large-scale tonal schemes within movements [demonstrate] a complete creative control over this all-important element of symphonic construction."[15] The parallel with Wagner is even deeper than Cooke allows. In order to achieve structural coherence in his later operas, Wagner designed individual acts as "continuous symphonies" in several movements.[16] The mature Mahler symphonies, although discontinuous, similarly demonstrate a complete creative control of large-scale tonal schemes *across* movements. This tonal mastery, coupled with a careful thematic design "tautly unifying a mass of multifarious detail,"[17] produces the overwhelming coherence and consistency that is the greatest testament to Mahler's genius.

Notes

Chapter 1

1. Arnold Schoenberg, *Berliner Tagebuch*, cited in Donald Mitchell, *The Wunderhorn Years* (London: Faber and Faber, 1975), 437.

2. Franz Loschnigg, "The Cultural Education of Gustav Mahler" (Ph.D. dissertation, University of Wisconsin-Madison, 1976), 43.

3. An exception is Gregory Proctor, "Technical Bases of Nineteenth-Century Chromatic Tonality" (Ph.D. dissertation, Princeton University, 1978).

4. Dika Newlin, *Bruckner, Mahler, Schoenberg*, 2nd ed. (New York: W. W. Norton, 1978), 129.

5. Hans Tischler, "Key Symbolism versus 'Progressive Tonality,' " *Musicology* 2 (1949): 383.

6. Ibid. 384.

7. Newlin, *Bruckner, Mahler, Schoenberg*, 129.

8. Ibid. 151-52.

9. Tischler, "Key Symbolism," 386-87.

10. Heinrich Schenker, *Free Composition*, 2 vols. (New York: Longman, 1979), vol. I, 11.

11. Ibid. 129. See also Harald Krebs, "Alternatives to Monotonality in Early Nineteenth-Century Music," *Journal of Music Theory* 25 (1981): 1-16.

12. See, for example, *Free Composition*, vol. I, 128 and 129, n. 6.

13. This useful and flexible term has been coined by Patrick McCreless in "Ernst Kurth and the Analysis of Chromatic Music of the Late Nineteenth Century," *Music Theory Spectrum* 5 (1983): 69.

14. Arnold Schoenberg, *Theory of Harmony* (Berkeley: University of California Press, 1978), 383-84.

15. Ibid. 153. Emphasis in the first paragraph is mine; that in the second paragraph is Schoenberg's.

16. Robert Bailey, "*Das Lied von der Erde*: Tonal Language and Formal Design." Paper read before the Forty-Fourth Annual Meeting of the American Musicological Society (21 October 1978). Emphasis is mine. The following description of the system is based upon Bailey's work as expressed in the five papers entered in the bibliography.

17. See, for example, Charles Rosen, *The Classical Style* (New York: W. W. Norton, 1972), 57-98 (especially, 83-95); and Rosen, *Sonata Forms* (New York: W. W. Norton, 1980), 246-49.

18. See Schenker, *Free Composition*, vol. I, 113-14.

19. Robert Bailey, *Tristan und Isolde: Prelude and "Transfiguration"* (New York: W. W. Norton, forthcoming).

20. Bailey, "*Das Lied*."

21. Heinrich Schenker, *Harmony* (Cambridge, Mass.: MIT Press, 1973), 189.

22. Schenker, *Kontrapunkt*, vol. I, 366, cited in *Harmony*, 188, note; and *Free Composition*, vol. I, 63.

23. Proctor, "Chromatic Tonality," iv.

24. Bailey, "*Das Lied*." See also Schoenberg, *Theory of Harmony*, 389.

25. Bailey, "*Tristan*."

26. Proctor, "Chromatic Tonality," 151.

27. Ibid. 131.

28. Ibid., 220.

29. Patrick McCreless, *Wagner's "Siegfried": Its Drama, History and Music* (Ann Arbor: UMI Research Press, 1982), 89.

30. Alma Mahler, *Memories and Letters*, ed. Donald Mitchell and Knud Martner, 3rd ed. (Seattle: University of Washington Press, 1975), 142.

31. Ibid. 152.

32. Ibid.

33. Loschnigg (458-66) makes a good case suggesting that the superstition was only in *Alma's* mind.

34. Gustav Mahler, *Selected Letters*, ed. Knud Martner (New York: Farrar, Strauss, Giroux, 1979), 341.

35. Bruno Walter, *Gustav Mahler* (New York: Greystone Press, 1941), 60.

36. Mahler, *Letters*, 347.

37. Ibid. 355.

38. According to Parks Grant, the first movement is in a different hand than the last three ("Mahler Editing and Research in Vienna," *Chord and Discord* 3 (1969): 102).

39. Mahler's revised orchestral score is in the collection of the Pierpont Morgan Library, New York.

40. H. G. Wells, *Experiment in Autobiography* (New York: MacMillan and Co., 1934), 161.

41. McCreless, "Ernst Kurth," 60.

42. See Diether de la Motte, "Das komplizierte Einfache: Zum ersten Satz der 9. Sinfonie von Gustav Mahler," *Musik und Bildung* 3 (1978): 150; Jack Diether, "The Expressive Content of Mahler's Ninth: An Interpretation," *Chord and Discord* 2 (1963): 78; and David Rivier, "A Note on Form in Mahler's Symphonies," *Chord and Discord* 2 (1954): 30.

43. See the photographic reproduction of the holograph of Mahler's orchestral draft, *IX. Symphonie: Partiturentwurf der ersten drei Sätze: Faksimile nach der Handschrift* (Vienna: Universal Edition, 1971), after I/54.

44. Diether, "Expressive Content," 96.

Chapter 2

1. Rosen, *Sonata Forms*, 222.

2. Musical examples are of three types: (1) *S.S.*: Quotations of the music itself in my own short score; (2) *Reduction*: Harmonic or melodic skeletons; and (3) *Sketch*: Interpretive voice-leading sketches. Measure numbers refer to the engraved score, unless preceded by "DS," in which case the reference is to the Draft Score. On p. 105 of the engraved score, the measures after 606 are incorrectly numbered.

3. Peter Andraschke, "Gustav Mahlers IX. Symphonie," *Beihefte zum Archiv für Musikwissenschaft* (Wiesbaden: Franz Steiner, 1976), 12.

4. See Andraschke, "Mahlers IX;" Diether, "Expressive Content;" and Carl Dahlhaus, "Form und Motiv in Mahlers IX Symphonie," *Neue Zeitschrift für Musik* 135 (1974): 296-99.

5. See, for example, Rivier, "A Note on Form," 29-33; and Erwin Ratz, "Zum Formproblem bei Gustav Mahler," *Musikforschung* 8 (1955): 169-77.

6. Motive "Y" is inserted between mm. 4 and 5 of the draft. See *Partiturentwurf*, I/1.

7. Schenker, *Free Composition*, vol. I, 134-38.

8. Rivier, "A Note on Form," 30.

9. Bailey, "*Das Lied*."

Chapter 3

1. Paul Bekker, *Gustav Mahlers Sinfonien* (Berlin: Schuster & Loeffler, 1921), 26.

2. The score identifies the *Ländler* and the last appearance of the waltz (see m. 406). The Draft Score, however, refers to the waltz tempo at m. DS 148 (later changed in pencil, then omitted entirely in the final version), and gives "Meno mosso subito (langsamer Menuett)" as the direction for the third dance (m. DS 298); the recurrence of this material at m. DS 394 is headed simply "Menuetto." Erwin Stein is perhaps the first commentator to refer to the three characters of the movement in these terms (in "Die Tempogestaltung in Mahlers IX. Symphonie," *Pult und Taktstock* 7 (November 1924): 111).

3. Andraschke, "Mahlers IX," 3. According to Stephen Hefling, this is the notebook which was owned by F. Charles Adler, and later by his widow. A complete transcription is given by Colin Matthews in his dissertation "Mahler At Work: Aspects of the Creative Process" (University of Sussex, 1977). See Stephen Hefling, "Variations *in nuce*: A Study of Mahler Sketches, and a Comment on Sketch Studies" in *Gustav Mahler Kolloquium 1979: Ein Bericht*, ed. Rudolf Klein (Kassel: Bärenreiter, 1981): 101–26; especially 122, n. 7.

4. Grant, "Mahler Research and Editing," 108 and 113.

5. Andraschke, "Mahlers IX," 4.

6. Michael Kennedy, *Mahler* (London, J. M. Dent & Sons Ltd., 1974), 149.

7. Stein, "Tempogestaltung," 111.

8. Hans Redlich, *Bruckner and Mahler* (London: J. M. Dent & Sons Ltd., 1954), 228.

9. Diether, "Expressive Content," 81.

10. Andraschke, "Mahlers IX," 63.

11. Ibid. 59.

12. John Williamson, review of Andraschke, *Music and Letters* 59 (1978): 213.

13. This chart is an amalgam of those given by Andraschke on pp. 60 and 64.

14. Andraschke, "Mahlers IX," p. 63.

15. See Rivier, "A Note on Form," 31; Diether, "Expressive Content," 82-83; and Andraschke, "Mahlers IX," 64.

16. Diether, "Expressive Content," 84.

17. The term "strophe" here designates a formal unit of several periods, but smaller than the

"section." Such a term is useful in discussion of very large movements, especially when, as is so often the case with Mahler, the repetitive, symmetrical vocal strophe serves as a model. See Robert Bailey, "From Song to Symphony and Back Again: Form and Tonal Language in Mahler's *Das Lied von der Erde*," *Nineteenth Century Music* (forthcoming).

18. Bekker, *Mahlers Sinfonien*, 30. (*Auch Mahlers Harmonik ist im einzelnen oft verblüffend naiv. . . . Dann wieder scheint sie unentwirrbar in ihrer krausen Verflechtung verschiedenartigster Klangelemente.*)

19. See Alma Mahler, *Memories and Letters*, 146-47; and Ernest Jones, *Sigmund Freud: Life and Work*, 3 vols. (London: Hogarth Press, 1955), vol. 2, 88-89.

20. Donald Mitchell, "Mahler and Freud," *Chord and Discord* 2 (1958): 66. Emphasis is mine.

21. See Warren Storey Smith, "Mahler Quotes Mahler," *Chord and Discord* 2 (1954): 7-13; and Diether, "Expressive Content," passim.

22. The chart is based on Andraschke's ("Mahlers IX," 60). Letter designations are those derived from my own analysis. There are two errors (typographical?) in Andraschke's chart: (1) No arrow should equate mm. DS 198-217 with the same measures of the final version—though thematically similar, the sections exhibit crucial differences; and (2) an arrow *should* equate mm. DS 455-546 with mm. 420-512.

23. Uncertain transcriptions are enclosed in brackets. The entry in the trombone staff (mm. DS 582-84) is apparently a sketch for a violin (II?) line. It is omitted from the transcription.

Chapter 4

1. Deryck Cooke, *Gustav Mahler* (Cambridge: Cambridge University Press, 1980), 117.

2. Douglass Green, *Form in Tonal Music*, 2nd ed. (New York: Holt, Rinehart and Winston, 1979), 166.

3. Rosen, *Sonata Forms*, 118-26.

4. See, for example, Schoenberg's derivation of this interpretation in *Theory of Harmony*, 246.

5. Kurt von Fischer, "Die Doppelschlagfigur in den zwei letzten Sätzen von Gustav Mahlers 9. Symphonie," *Archiv für Musikwissenschaft* 32 (1975): 100-101.

Chapter 5

1. "*Die letzten Sätze sind die Klippe, ich werde mich hüten, ich schreibe nur einsätzige Symphonien.*" (Cosima Wagner, *Tagebücher*, 2 vols. (Munich: R. Piper Verlag, 1977), vol. II: 827.)

2. Paul Bekker, *Die Sinfonie von Beethoven bis Mahler* (Berlin: Schuster & Loeffler, n.d.), 13-15.

3. Frank Wohlfahrt, *Die Geschichte der Sinfonie* (Hamburg: Verlag der Musikhandlung K. D. Wagner, 1966), 41-42.

4. Bekker, *Mahlers Sinfonien*, 41-42. The best example is the Beethoven Seventh.

5. For a provocative discussion of this idea in a more general sense, see Saul Novack, "Some Thoughts on the Nature of Musical Composition," *Current Musicology* 6 (1968): 100-105.

6. Paul Bekker, *Beethoven* (London: J. M. Dent, 1927), 76.

7. Robert Bailey, "Form and Musical Language in Brahms's Fourth Symphony." Paper read before the International Brahms Congress (April 1980).

8. Bekker, *Mahlers Sinfonien*, 19. (*"Was dem ersten Satz zum Vorteil gereichte: jenes Fehlen des Zielbewusstseins, des logischen Müssens sowohl in der Anlage des Ganzen wie in der Gestaltung der einzelnen Themen, das eben wurde dem Finale zum Verhängnis. . . . Hier jedoch versagte Bruckner."*) Dika Newlin seems to find the finales entirely satisfactory, but she considers the goal of attaining "inter-relationship of movements" to be sufficiently satisfied by numerous citations of themes from earlier movements (see Newlin, *Bruckner, Mahler, Schoenberg*, 96).

9. Bailey, "From Song to Symphony and Back Again."

10. Bekker, *Mahlers Sinfonien*, p. 20. (*"Das Finale, mag es kurz, mag es lang sein, mag es . . . ein weitgesponnenes Allegro . . . oder ein ruhevolles Adagio . . . alle diese Finale . . . sind das Zentrum, zu dem die Fäden sämtlicher vorangehender Sätze hinleiten."*)

11. Mahler so designated symphonic sections comprising one large movement or several smaller ones. See, for example, the score to the Third.

12. Bekker, *Mahlers Sinfonien*, 22-23.

13. Colin Matthews, "Mahler at Work: Some Observations on the IX and X Symphony Sketches," *Soundings* 4 (1974). This is the notebook referred to by Andraschke and Hefling (see chapter 3, n. 3).

14. Mahler himself used the same metaphor for symphonic structure, referring to his Second, in a letter of April 1895 to Oskar Bie: "How much I regret having been able to offer no more than the exposition of a work to such a man as yourself—for exposition is what these three movements are, as you will scarcely have failed to realized." (Mahler, *Letters*, 160.) Cosima reports that Wagner spoke of not being "obliged to compose in four movements . . . if one shaped the motives—first, second, return to the first—into movements." (Cosima Wagner, *Diaries*, 2 vols. [New York: Harcourt Brace Jovanovich, 1980], II:174.)

15. Cooke, *Gustav Mahler*, 15.

16. See Robert Bailey, "The Structure of the *Ring* and its Evolution," *Nineteenth Century Music* 1 (1977): 59-60; and Patrick McCreless, *Wagner's "Siegfried,"* 188-94.

17. Cooke, *Gustav Mahler*, 13.

Bibliography

Scores

Mahler, Gustav. *Symphonie Nr. 9*. Revised edition, Vienna: Universal Edition, 1969.
_____. *IX. Symphonie: Partiturentwurf der ersten drei Sätze: Faksimile nach der Handschrift*. Vienna: Universal Edition, 1971.

Other Sources Cited

Andraschke, Peter. *Gustav Mahlers IX. Symphonie: Kompositionsprozess und Analyse. Beihefte zum Archive für Musikwissenschaft*. Wiesbaden: Franz Steiner, 1976.
Bailey, Robert. "*Das Lied von der Erde*: Tonal Language and Formal Design." Paper read before the Forty-Fourth Annual Meeting of the American Musicological Society, 21 October 1978.
_____. "From Song to Symphony and Back Again: Form and Tonal Language in Mahler's Fourth Symphony and *Das Lied von der Erde*." *Nineteenth Century Music*, forthcoming.
_____. "Form and Musical Language in Brahms's Fourth Symphony." Paper read before The International Brahms Congress, April 1980.
_____. "The Structure of the *Ring* and Its Evolution." *Nineteenth Century Music* 1 (1977): 48-61.
_____. *Tristan und Isolde: Prelude and "Transfiguration."* New York: W. W. Norton, forthcoming.
Bekker, Paul. *Beethoven*. London: J. M. Dent, 1927.
_____. *Gustav Mahlers Sinfonien*. Berlin: Schuster und Loeffler, 1921.
_____. *Die Sinfonie von Beethoven bis Mahler*. Berlin: Schuster & Loeffler, n.d.
Cooke, Deryck. *Gustav Mahler: An Introduction to his Music*. Cambridge: Cambridge University Press, 1980.
Dahlhaus, Carl. "Form und Motiv in Mahlers IX Symphonie." *Neue Zeitschrift für Musik* 135 (1974): 296-99.
de la Motte, Diether. "Das komplizierte Einfache: Zum ersten Satz der 9. Sinfonie von Gustav Mahler." *Musik und Bildung* 3 (1978): 145-51.
Diether, Jack. "The Expressive Content of Mahler's Ninth: An Interpretation." *Chord and Discord* 2 (1963): 69-107.
Fischer, Kurt von. "Die Doppelschlagfigur in den zwei letzten Sätzen von Gustav Mahlers 9. Symphonie." *Archiv für Musikwissenschaft* 32 (1975): 99-105.
Grant, Parks. "Mahler Research and Editing in Vienna." *Chord and Discord* 3 (1969): 101-15.
Green, Douglass. *Form in Tonal Music*. 2nd ed. New York: Holt Rinehart & Winston, 1979.
Hefling, Steven. "Variations *in nuce*: A Study of Mahler Sketches, and a Comment on Sketch

Studies." In *Gustav Mahler Kolloquium 1979: Ein Bericht*, pp. 102-26. Edited by Rudolf Klein. Kassel: Bärenreiter, 1981.

Jones, Ernest. *Sigmund Freud: Life and Work*. 3 vols. London: Hogarth Press, 1955.

Kennedy, Michael. *Mahler*. London: J. M. Dent and Sons Ltd., 1974.

Krebs, Harald. "Alternatives to Monotonality in Early Nineteenth-Century Music." *Journal of Music Theory* **25** (1981): 1-16.

Loschnigg, Franz. "The Cultural Education of Gustav Mahler." Ph.D. dissertation, University of Wisconsin-Madison, 1976.

Mahler, Alma Maria. *Memories and Letters*. Edited by Donald Mitchell and Knud Martner, translated by Basil Creighton. 3rd ed. Seattle: University of Washington Press, 1975.

Mahler, Gustav. *Selected Letters*. Edited by Knud Martner, translated by Eithne Wilkins and Ernst Kaiser. New York: Farrar Strauss Giroux, 1979.

Matthews, Colin. "Mahler at Work: Some Observations on the IX and X Symphony Sketches." *Soundings* **4** (1974): 76-86.

McCreless, Patrick. "Ernst Kurth and the Analysis of the Chromatic Music of the Late Nineteenth Century." *Music Theory Spectrum* **5** (1983): 56-75.

_____. *Wagner's "Siegfried": Its Drama, History and Music*. Ann Arbor: UMI Research Press, 1982.

Mitchell, Donald. *Gustav Mahler: The Wunderhorn Years*. London: Faber and Faber, 1975.

_____. "Mahler and Freud." *Chord and Discord* **2** (1963): 63-68.

Newlin, Dika. *Bruckner, Mahler, Schoenberg*. 2nd ed. New York: W.W. Norton, 1978.

Novack, Saul. "Some Thoughts on the Nature of Musical Composition." *Current Musicology* **6** (1968): 100-105.

Proctor, Gregory. *Technical Bases of Nineteenth-Century Chromatic Tonality*. Ph.D. dissertation, Princeton University, 1978.

Ratz, Erwin. "Zum Formproblem bei Gustav Mahler." *Musikforschung* **8** (1955): 169-77.

Redlich, Hans F. *Bruckner and Mahler*. London: Dent, 1954.

Rivier, David. "A Note on Form in Mahler's Symphonies." *Chord and Discord* **2/7** (1954): 29-33.

Rosen, Charles. *The Classical Style*. New York: W. W. Norton, 1972.

_____. *Sonata Forms*. New York: W. W. Norton, 1980.

Schenker, Heinrich. *Free Composition*. Translated by Ernst Oster. 2 vols. New York: Longman, 1979.

_____. *Harmony*. Edited by Oswald Jonas, translated by Elisabeth Mann Borgese. Cambridge, Mass.: MIT Press, 1973.

Schoenberg, Arnold. *Theory of Harmony*. Translated by Roy E. Carter. Berkeley: University of California Press, 1978.

Smith, Warren Storey. "Mahler Quotes Mahler." *Chord and Discord* **2** (1954): 7-13.

Stein, Erwin. "Die Tempogestaltung in Mahlers IX. Symphony." *Pult und Taktstock* **1** (1924): 97-99 and 111-14.

Tischler, Hans. "Key Symbolism vs. 'Progressive Tonality.' " *Musicology* **2** (1949): 383-88.

Wagner, Cosima. *Diaries*. Translated by Geoffrey Skelton. 2 vols. New York: Harcourt Brace Jovanovich, 1980.

_____. *Tagebücher*. Munich: R. Piper Verlag, 1977.

Walter, Bruno. *Gustav Mahler*. Translated by James Galston. New York: Greystone Press, 1941.

Williamson, John. Review of: *Gustav Mahlers IX Symphonie*, by Peter Andraschke. *Music and Letters* **59** (1978): 211-14.

Wohlfahrt, Frank. *Die Geschichte der Sinfonie*. Hamburg: Verlag der Musikhandlung K. D. Wagner, 1966.

Index

Abteilung, 5, 103, 105, 124 n.11
Adagio-symphony, 102-3
Added-sixth chord, 6, 21
Adler, F. Charles, 122 n.3
Andante Comodo, 10-11
   Coda, 39, 40-41
   Development, 21-34, 34, 35-36
   Exposition, 14-21, 23
      First Tonal Area, 15-17, 22, 23, 25, 26, 31, 34
      Introduction, 14-15, 21
      second theme, 16, 25, 40
      Second Tonal Area, 18-21, 29-30, 31
      Transition, 17-18, 18, 37
   and *Ländler*, 57
   Recapitulation, 18, 19, 23, 34, 37-41
      First Tonal Area, 37-38, 39
      Second Tonal Area, 38-39
   Retransition, 25, 27, 31, 34-37
   and *Rondo-Burleske*, 89-90, 92
   tonal plot summarized, 14, 15, 21-22, 34, 37-38, 41-42, 90
Andraschke, Peter, 14, 43, 45, 57
Apotheosis-Finale, 101
Augmented triad, 78, 82. *See also* Motto progression; Symmetrical subdivision; Third-relations

Background. *See* Ursatz
Bailey, Robert, 4, 5-6, 7, 34
Bassbrechung. See Ursatz
Beethoven, Ludwig van, 101, 101-2
Bekker, Paul, 43, 54, 101, 102
Bie, Oskar, 124 n.14
Brahms, Johannes, 101, 102
Bruckner, Anton, 43, 102, 124 n.8

Chromaticism, 7-8. *See also* Modal interchange
Coda. *See Andante Comodo:* Coda; *Rondo-Burleske:* Codas

Common practice. *See* Tonality, common-practice
Concentric tonality. *See* Tonality, concentric
Cooke, Deryck, 117
Counterpoint, invertible, 81
Counterpoint, quadruple, 78
Cross-reference. *See* Motivic cross-reference; Tonal cross-reference

Dance types, 43, 45, 50, 122 n.2. *See also Ländler* (dance)
Das Lied von der Erde (Mahler), 5-6, 34, 109
Development. See *Andante Comodo:* Development
Diether, Jack, 44, 50
Displacement, D/D-flat
   across movements, 104
   in Finale, 106, 107-8, 110, 110, 114
   in *Rondo-Burleske*, 88-89, 95, 96, 99
Displacement, metric, 31-32, 66, 73, 90
Displacement, 6-5
   in *Andante Comodo*, 27, 41
   implying double tonic, 15, 75, 92, 106, 112
   in modulation, 24, 28
   at several levels, 16, 25
Divider, 5, 51, 62, 80, 83
Dominant. *See also* Interruption; Structural dominant
   avoidance of, 17, 31, 31, 39, 80
   in foreground, 15, 20, 25, 33, 54, 68, 70
   implied, 74, 93, 113-14
   middleground, 52, 68
Dominant substitute, 74, 93
Double-tonic complex, 4-6. *See also* Fluctuating tonality; Modal interchange; Paired tonics; Suspended tonality; Third-relations; Tonality, progressive
   common elements, 69-70, 78, 108, 111-12, 114
   juxtaposed elements, 28, 37, 70, 80-81, 92, 94-95, 97, 106

Index

and modulation, 19
from neighbor motion, 14-15, 15-16, 20-21, 27, 34-37, 90, 106
by overlay of textures, 19, 29-31, 52, 63, 70-73, 75-77, 87, 87-88, 90-92
resolution of, 37-39, 40-41, 59, 109, 116-17
reversal of elements, 17, 18, 77
and structural dominant, 5, 7, 8, 14
surface implications, 6, 66-67
and tonal plot, 21, 22, 23, 27, 34, 41-42, 63, 88
and tonal structure, 5-6, 7-8, 14, 18, 102
Draft Score
dance types in, 122 n.2
and final version, 46, 51-52, 57
history, 8-9
revisions, 9
to *Andante Comodo*, 21, 121 n.6
to *Ländler*, 43-44, 50, 51-52, 57-63

Episode. *See* Finale, of GM's IX; *Rondo-Burleske*; Rondo elements
Exposition. *See Andante Comodo*

Finale, of GM's IX
Coda, 115-17
Episode 1, 108
Episode 2, 111-14
foreshadowed, 50, 68, 89-90
Refrain 1, 106-8
Refrain 2, 109-11
Refrain 3, 114-15
and *Rondo-Burleske*, 68, 104
tonal plot, 11, 96, 105-6, 116-17
Finale, symphonic, 101-3, 105-6, 124 n.8, 124 n.14
Finale-symphony, 102, 103
Fluctuating tonality, 4
Fundamental structure. *See Ursatz*

Grant, Parks, 121 n.38

Harmonielehre. See Theory of Harmony (Schoenberg)
Harmony, 54-55, 65, 66-67, 70, 71, 73, 109. *See also* Dominant; Modulation techniques
Hefling, Stephen, 122 n.3

Interruption, 22, 24. *See also* Dominant
Irony, musical, 33, 54

Kennedy, Michael, 44
Key-symbolism, 2

Ländler (dance), 43, 45. *See also* Dance types
Ländler (movement), 9, 11, 44-47. *See also* Draft Score

Ländler 1, 47-49
Ländler return, 57-63
minuets, 43, 46, 47-48, 50-51, 62
and *Rondo-Burleske*, 84, 96
tonal plot
in Draft, 57-59
in final version, 47-48, 50-51, 51, 52, 57, 63
waltzes, 43, 44, 46-47, 82, 85, 96, 104-5
Waltz-trio 1, 50, 52-55
Waltz-trio 2, 50-51, 55-56
Waltz-trio 3, 50, 51-52, 55-57
Lied elements, 10-11, 22
"Lockung" (Schoenberg), 4, 5

McCreless, Patrick, 119 n.13
Mahler, Gustav
Das Lied von der Erde, 5-6, 34, 109
harmonic technique. *See* Dominant; Double-tonic complex; Harmony; Modulation techniques; Structural dominant; Tonality, progressive
symphonic design, 117, 124 n.14
Symphony I, 54
Symphony II, 2-3, 54, 103
Symphony III, 5, 54
Symphony IV, 5, 102-3
Symphony V, 2
Symphony IX, 8-9, 9-11, 43. *See also Andante Comodo;* Draft score; Finale, of GM's IX; *Ländler* (movement); *Rondo-Burleske;* Sketches
tonal plot, 9, 104-5, 116-17
Symphony X, 43
Major thirds. *See* Motto theme; Symmetrical subdivision; Third relations
Matthews, Colin, 104, 122 n.3
Minuet. *See Ländler* (movement): minuets
Modal interchange
chromatic mode, 7, 17, 40
to clarify double tonic, 6, 62, 73, 92
to clarify tonic, 6, 63, 112-13
and the dominant, 39, 97
in double tonic, 52, 58
to modulate, 83
for structural contrast, 105
in structural elements, 15, 17, 18, 20, 21, 35
Mode. *See* Modal interchange
Modulation techniques, 17-18, 18-19, 23, 24-25, 28, 31, 56, 85
Motivic cross-reference, 5, 9, 28-29, 50, 102, 124 n.8. *See also* Tonal cross-reference
Motto progression. *See also* Motto theme; Symmetrical subdivision
and D/D-flat displacement, 110, 114
and design of GM's IX, 96, 103
in Finale, 109, 115

in *Ländler,* 54, 55, 57
in *Rondo-Burleske,* 84, 87, 94
source, 32, 50
Motto theme, 50, 61, 104, 106, 109. *See also* Motto progression

Newlin, Dika, 1-2, 3, 124 n.8. *See also* Tonality, progressive
Ninth chord. *See* Seventh chord

Operatic structure, 2, 117
Orchesterlied, Op. 8/5 (Schoenberg), 4

Paired tonics, 3-8, 18. *See also* Double-tonic complex
Partiturentwurf. See Draft Score
Plagal prolongation
 foreground, 31, 73, 75, 115
 middleground, 39, 48, 48-49, 69
Proctor, Gregory, 7, 8
Progressive tonality. *See* Tonality, progressive

Quotation, of GM by GM, 54

Recapitulation, 105, 124 n.14. *See also Andante Comodo;* Recapitulation
Redlich, Hans, 44
Refrain, 22-23, 25, 37, 65. *See also Andante Comodo:* Development; Finale, of GM's IX; *Rondo-Burleske;* Rondo elements
Revisions. *See* Draft Score: revisions
Rivier, David, 50
Rondo-Burleske
 Codas, 98-99
 Episode 1, 82-85, 95-96
 Episode 2, 85-89, 96
 Episode 3, 66, 80, 89-96, 104
 episodes as trios, 82, 85, 96
 Refrain 1, 67-77, 95, 96-98
 Refrain 2, 77-82, 95
 Refrain 3, 82, 96-99
 tonal plot, 11, 65, 67-68, 68, 77-78, 84, 95-96
Rondo elements, 10-11, 22, 65, 82, 105
Rosen, Charles, 13, 18

Schenker, Heinrich, 3, 6
Schoenberg, Arnold, 1, 4, 5, 120 n.24, 123 n.4
Schubert, Franz, 43
Seventh chord, 6, 68, 113-14
Six-four chord, 74, 93
Sketches, 8, 43, 103-4, 122 n.3
Sonata form, 13-14, 21-22, 22, 41, 65, 101
 as symphonic paradigm, 105, 124 n.14
Stein, Erwin, 44, 122 n.2
Stichvorlage, 9, 43, 121 n.38

Strophe, 122 n.17
Structural dissonance, 13, 18, 37, 104
Structural dominant
 and double-tonic complex, 5, 7, 8
 in GM's IX, 22, 24, 39-40, 41
 in sonata form, 13-14
Subdominant. *See* Plagal prolongation
Suspended tonality, 4
Symmetrical subdivision. *See also* Motto progression
 by major thirds, 7-8
 background, 21, 41
 foreground, 27, 57, 67, 69, 80, 82, 83
 middleground, 84, 89
 by other intervals, 8, 88
Symphony, 101-3, 105, 124 n.14

Thematic cross-reference. *See* Motivic cross-reference
Theory of Harmony (Schoenberg), 3-4, 120 n.24, 123 n.4
Third-relations. *See also* Double-tonic complex; Motto progression; Symmetrical subdivision
 background, 21, 34, 41-42, 46, 50, 51
 in double-tonic complex, 5, 7
 foreground, 27, 40, 68, 84-85
 middleground, 68, 108, 114-15
Thirds, major. *See* Motto theme; Symmetrical subdivision
Tischler, Hans, 1-2
Tonal area. *See Andante Comodo:* Exposition
Tonal cross-reference, 5, 9, 102-4. *See also* Motivic cross-reference
Tonality, common-practice, 2-3, 8, 13-14, 21-22, 101, 102, 106
Tonality, concentric, 2, 3
Tonality, fluctuating, 4
Tonality, progressive, 1-2, 2-3
Tonality, suspended, 4
Tonal plot, 3, 41, 102-3. *See also Andante Comodo;* Finale, of GM's IX; *Ländler* (movement); *Rondo-Burleske*
 of GM's II, 3, 103
 of GM's IV, 5, 102-3
 of GM's IX, 9, 104-5, 116-17
Transition. *See Andante Comodo:* Exposition
Trio, 43. *See also Ländler* (movement): waltzes
Tristan und Isolde (Wagner), 4, 5
Tritone, 8, 35

Ursatz, 2-3, 8, 13-14, 41. *See also* Structural dominant

Variations, 11, 101
"Voll jener Susse" (Schoenberg), 4

Wagner, Richard, 2, 4, 5, 101, 117, 124 n.14
Walter, Bruno, 9
Waltz. *See Ländler* (movement): waltzes
Wells, Herbert George, 9
Whole-tone scale, 88